P9-CQQ-631

Leadership for Mortals

Leadership for Mortals

Developing and sustaining
leaders of learning

Dean Fink

P·C·P
Paul Chapman
Publishing

CORWIN
PRESS

© Dean Fink 2005

First published 2005

Apart from any fair dealing for the purposes of
research or private study, or criticism or review, as
permitted under the Copyright, Designs and
Patents Act, 1988, this publication may be
reproduced, stored or transmitted, in any form or
by any means, only with the prior permission in
writing of the publishers, or in the case of
reprographic reproduction, in accordance with the
terms of licences issued by the Copyright
Licensing Agency. Enquiries concerning
reproduction outside those terms should be sent
to the publishers.

Paul Chapman Publishing
A SAGE Publications Company
1 Oliver's Yard
55 City Road
 London EC1Y 1SP

SAGE Publications Inc
2455 Teller Road
Thousand Oaks, California 91320

SAGE Publications India Pvt Ltd
B-42, Panchsheel Enclave
Post Box 4109
New Delhi 110 017

Library of Congress Control Number: 2005920923

A catalogue record for this book is available from
the British Library

ISBN 1-4129-0053-0
ISBN 1-4129-0054-9 (pbk)

Typeset by Dorwyn Ltd, Wells, Somerset
Printed in Great Britain by T.J. International, Padstow, Cornwall

To Louise Stoll and Andy Hargreaves

Your help, friendship and encouragement have made my third age
a joyous and stimulating adventure

Contents

Acknowledgments

To express my appreciation to all the individuals who have helped me over the years to assemble the material for this book would require a separate book. I've therefore identified a few specific people and groups of friends and colleagues in the hope that I have included everyone in one way or the other. I am indebted to all my former colleagues with the Halton Board of Education, particularly Wayne Burns and Garry Crossman, for nurturing my leadership aspirations and providing me with excellent models of leaders of learning. To my former colleagues of the Thursday breakfast club who are among the finest educational leaders I have ever encountered, your collective example has deepened my understanding of leadership in action. To the thousands of school leaders in many different countries that I have encountered in the past ten years, I am inspired by your example of courage and perseverance in the face of challenging and often contradictory expectations, and to the many academics that have assisted my growth as a public scholar I remain in awe of your wisdom and humbled by how much there is to learn. To Brent Davies, your support and friendship have opened many doors for me.

I am particularly appreciative of the friendship of Corrie Giles, Carol Brayman, Jane Creasy, Andy Hargreaves, Louise Stoll and Paul Chung who have read some or all of the manuscript. Your advice was invaluable, even when I didn't take it. I, of course, take sole responsibility for the contents of the book. Marianne Lagrange, together with Sage Publications and Alma Harris, the general editor, has also provided enormous help and support.

To my family, as always, your love and encouragement keep me going. To my mother, Marjorie, your energy and optimism are a daily inspiration. You have certainly proven that age is a state of mind. To my daughters, Danielle and Tracy, who I am proud to say have followed in their father's professional footsteps, your daily adventures keep me grounded in reality. To my young learners, Zachary and Riley, you keep me connected to the purposes of education and to my love of teaching, and to my wife, Ramona, your love, support, and fortitude throughout the years have made any successes that I may have had, or will have, possible.

Every effort has been made to trace and acknowledge all the copyright owners of the material reprinted herein. However, if any copyright owners have not been located and contacted at the time of publication, the publishers will be pleased to make the necessary arrangements at the first opportunity.

Foreword

It seems that no modern concept has been more powerfully received in the consciousness of those concerned with school reform and improvement than leadership. The contemporary literature highlights and reinforces the importance of leadership in generating and sustaining school development and change. Effective leadership, primarily in the guise of the head-teacher, has long been identified with school success. Over the last three decades, the sheer volume of literature on the subject has grown and leadership is centre stage in efforts to transform schooling.

Yet, those who write about leadership do so from many different perspectives and traditions resulting sometimes in competing, if not contradictory messages about successful leadership practice. Also, some of the books about leadership fail to fully engage with its human dimension and avoid dealing with the messy, complex emotional terrain that inevitably faces all leaders whatever their context or position. 'Leadership for Mortals' is a welcome departure from this trend. Not only does it give leadership a voice but it acknowledges the centrality of certain human values and qualities that shape the leadership endeavor.

This book is both refreshing and rare because Dean Fink draws upon his own leadership practice to reflect upon and illuminate the realities of leading schools and schools systems. His forty years as a practicing school and school district leader in Ontario plus his ten years as a consultant and academic provides a unique and powerful backdrop for a contemporary tour around leadership theory and practice. One of his main messages is that leadership does not require superhuman heroes; rather he suggests that most of us have the capacity to assume an important direct or indirect leadership role through the appropriateness of our invitations to others. Leadership, he suggests is everywhere, it is not the preserve of one individual but is a form of collective influence which involves the many rather than the few.

The book focuses on the centrality of core values that shape leadership practice. It explores the potential of personal invitation, trust, integrity, respect and optimism as fundamental components of successful leadership. Through examples, stories and reflections the book illuminates and celebrates the human dimension of leading. The book explores the way in which reason, ethics, common sense, imagination and intuition interplay to create an intricate personal tapestry of leadership knowledge and understanding. There are no tips for leaders in this book, no toolkits, checklists or competences. Instead, attention is paid to the challenges of leadership that go beyond the superficial 'designer leadership' to address the deep moral issues that face all leaders in schools or school systems at some time.

Fink suggests that successful leaders make connections by developing firm knowledge by: understanding of their context; developing political acumen; understanding learning; critical thinking; making connections; futures thinking and developing emotional understanding. Each of these is explored in the book along with the central issue of how leadership is nurtured and sustained, particularly in the most difficult contexts. The final section of the book deals with the trajectories of leadership – inbound, outbound, peripheral, insider and boundary trajectories, in other words the ways in which leadership interfaces and connects both within and outside the organization. It also deals with the important issue of succession and how potential leaders are identified and recruited pointing to the fact that serendipity often plays a major role in successful leadership succession.

In the opening section of the book, Dean Fink says 'I hope the academy will deem this book to be respectable'. Given that the academy has produced many books that simply have not succeeded in bringing together leadership theory and practice in any meaningful way, possibly they are not best placed to judge. Following September 11, Rudolph W Giuliani wrote, 'Leadership does not happen. It can be taught, learned, developed. Ultimately you will know what techniques and approaches work best – those you hope to lead will tell you. Much of your ability to get people to do what they have to do is going to depend on what they perceive when they look at you and listen to you. They need to see someone who is stronger than they are, but human too.'

Leadership for Mortals reminds us that leaders are human too and that leadership is fundamentally about values, principles and ethics. It challenges many of the traditional beliefs about leadership, particularly superhero leadership, to bring us back to the reality of leadership as individual connection and personal compassion. This is not a book to put on your shelf but one to read and re-read to ensure the moral purpose and human dimension of leadership are not forgotten.

Alma Harris

Introduction

Developing and sustaining leaders of learning

I've read a lot of books and articles on leadership over the past forty years. Some of these works have been wonderfully informative and inspirational, some have been patronizing drivel, and others so turgid and filled with exclusionary language that they left me clueless as to what the authors were talking about. Regardless of type, virtually all the authors began their efforts with an explanation of their reasons for writing about leadership and why they felt qualified to do so. So! Why am I writing a book on leadership and what qualifications do I bring to the task? I have contributed chapters and articles here and there on leadership, but the obvious answer is that I've never written a book exclusively on leadership before. Now, after forty years as a practising school and school district leader, and ten years as a consultant working with leaders in over 30 different countries, I'm confident that I have learned something useful about educational leadership that present and prospective leaders might find helpful and even motivating.

I hope the academy will deem this book to be respectable. To that end I will call extensively on the work of international leadership scholars, my own recent research, and that of others. I have, however, written this book first and foremost for practising and prospective leaders. The renowned Canadian novelist and teacher W.O. Mitchell always advised potential writers to find their own voice. The 'voice' in this book is the same 'voice' that I have used to conduct my many seminars with practitioners over the years. If the book has a conversational tone and is easily accessible then I have succeeded. I've also employed endnotes rather than APA style to maintain the flow of my narrative and to make this work more comprehensible for busy leaders in schools and districts. In some ways this book is autobio-graphical because leadership is a very personal thing, and one's view of leadership reflects 'who' you are, 'what' you are, and 'where' you are in time and space. Since I like to tell stories that connect leader-ship insights to my personal experiences and those of international colleagues, pose thought provoking questions, and employ humour and case studies to illustrate ideas and concepts in my seminars, I have included these approaches in the pages that follow.

What really inspires me to spend the time and energy to write this book, however, is my conviction that the contemporary state of education internationally, and of educational leadership in particu-lar, limits student learning, stultifies teacher creativity and profes-sionalism, and discourages people that have the ability and passion to lead our schools and educate our children for the emerging knowledge society.[1] Ironically, leadership within the present inter-national policy context has become a growth industry. Politicians demand more of it, academics decry the lack of it, and potential school leaders are deciding 'to hell with it'. A combination of disen-chantment with leadership roles as a result of the standards/stan-dardisation agenda, and demographic changes as the baby boom generation moves on, have produced, and will continue to produce, a rapid turnover of school heads and other educational leaders in the schools of most Western educational jurisdictions.[2] I would submit that we are making the business of leadership so complicated that we seem to need 'super heroes' to run a school.

In fact as I look back on my own leadership career, I am amazed that I did as well as I did considering that many of my decisions and actions were based on intuition, common sense, acquired experi-ence, reason and fairly strong convictions about what constituted good and ethical practice. I often had to make decisions without all the evidence available and hope that my instincts were accurate. I did not, however, have to conform to the 'laundry lists' of 'best' practices that plague contemporary leaders, or measure up to the latest leadership model 'du jour'. Like most educational leaders and potential leaders, I was not heroic, particularly charismatic, or even uniquely visionary. But with guidance from my mentors, consider-able training, experience, and careful succession planning, I was rea-sonably successful. Because most of us involved in educational leadership are just ordinary people who are just trying to do the best we can with the tools that we were born with, I have chosen *Leadership for Mortals* as the title for this book.

As I reflect on my years as an educational leader, I marvel at my good fortune. I found each of my various leadership roles personally rewarding and professionally enriching. I would like to think that we can recapture, or in some cases capture, the kind of passion for educational leadership that most of my contemporaries and I brought to our work. The overriding intention of this book, therefore, is in some small way to inspire practising leaders and potential leaders to renew their commitment to and enthusiasm for educational leadership and leading for learning. This is the reason for the subtitle, *Developing and sustaining leaders of learning*.

Chapter 1, *Challenge*, sets the scene for the book by describing the policy environment within which existing and potential school leaders currently operate. For many in the academic community this explanation will not be new, but as a historian I find it useful to contextualise my leadership model 'for mortals' in both time and space. Historically, changes in education have moved at a glacial pace and have tended to nibble around the edges. Critics of education when I was a practising leader contended that it took 15 years from the time an idea was initiated until it was implemented in schools. Substantive changes inevitably foundered on bureaucratic inertia, political timidity, community nostalgia, and teacher resistance. The organisational structures of most schools around the world are fundamentally unchanged since the beginning of the century – the twentieth century that is. I'm always astonished at the similarity between the contemporary secondary schools that I visit internationally, and the school I attended as a student, and the schools I taught in as a young teacher in the 1960s; they are for the most part hierarchical, bureaucratised and balkanised.[3]

While the historical structures have remained intact, recent policy efforts by governments usually described as 'New Public Management' have attempted to focus schools' efforts on results as opposed to inputs and processes through the use of market forces, standardised high stakes testing, and stringent curriculum requirements. These policies have placed unique pressures on leaders, and in the process undermined educational leadership and replaced it with a form of instrumental managerialism that undercuts the very purposes of schools. While 'New Public Management' can claim short-term gains, large questions remain as to its efficacy in sustaining important changes over time. As a result, a third form of public policy dialogue that focuses on organisations as 'learning communities' has emerged. A learning community aims to enhance the learning of all the participants in an organisation as a way to advance and sustain its purposes. Moving schools in this direction will require leaders who are 'leaders of learning' who can engage their colleagues in a shared commitment to improve the learning opportunities for all students. For contemporary leaders, dealing with the fallout from 'New Public Management' while developing their schools as learning communities creates unprecedented but not impossible challenges.

Within this policy context, the remaining chapters of the book outline and develop what I consider to be a realistic model of leadership that puts forward a way to develop and sustain existing and potential leaders that does not require superhuman heroes, self-sacrificing martyrs or compliant government messengers.

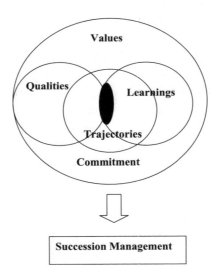

Figure 1.

Figure 1 visually captures the five components of the model developed in this book, that I believe have the potential to provide a structure for succession management within educational jurisdictions, that can connect the identification, recruitment, preparation, selection, and on-going professional growth of educational leaders to become leaders of learning in their schools and school districts.

For most of my career in state education in the Canadian province of Ontario, I have held some kind of leadership role. While it may sound simplistic and perhaps naïve, I always believed and acted on the premise that my job as a leader was to ensure the learning of the students in my care. If this meant mobilising community support for the school, raising funds to purchase computers, dismissing an incompetent teacher, modelling good classroom practices, taking on the district office on behalf of my school, or supporting a troubled colleague, it all added up to my trying to create a situation that enhanced the learning of my students. These activities were means to an end, not ends in themselves. It seems to me that there is only one purpose for school leaders and that is to enhance the learning of students. I constantly challenge leaders to ask one question of their schools' decisions, practices, customs or policies – do they enhance the learning of their students? This question powerfully focuses attention on what matters in a school. The very best of the thousands of educational leaders with whom I have interacted over the years were, and most still are, passionately, creatively, obsessively and steadfastly committed to enhancing 'deep' learning for students – learning for understanding, learning for life, learning for a knowledge society. It is this overriding dedication to 'deep' learning for students that is at the very heart of *Leadership for Mortals*, which I describe in Chapter 2 – *Commitment*.

In the past ten years I have had the good fortune to visit with school leaders in many different countries who are doing a magnificent job of leading learning for all their students in far more challenging conditions than I had ever experienced in my leadership career. There is Jane in Australia, for example, who heads up one of the most challenging schools in New South Wales, with quiet dignity, passion, and effectiveness. Then there is Allan who has turned a gang-ridden school in the heart of the most troubled section of Belfast into an oasis of safety and learning. Elena in Piscu in Romania, is the principal of a small school in a pre-industrial village, who inspires her staff daily to achieve great things with children, with virtually no support from government, and infrequent pay cheques. Then there is Charmaine in Ontario who refuses to adopt quick fix remedies for the language problems of her racially and ethnically diverse school. She has challenged her staff to promote literacy across the curriculum, and in the process raised her school's achievement on the provincial 'high-stakes' literacy test from below the median to second place in her very large school district – ahead of all but one of the middle-class schools in the leafy suburbs.

Nice stories, but what is the point? Leaders of learning such as those described, come in all shapes and sizes, genders, races, religions, backgrounds and contexts. These are not heroes, or even people uniquely blessed by the Almighty with leadership abilities, although they have these capacities in abundance. Rather they are ordinary people who through extraordinary commitment, effort, and determination have become extraordinary, and have made the people around them exceptional. Educational leadership is more art than science; it is more about character than technique; it is more about inspiration than charisma; it is more about leading student and teacher learning than the management of things.

Rudy Giuliani, the Mayor of New York at the time of the Twin Towers disaster stated, "Great leaders lead by ideas." I would alter this slightly and add – "Great leaders lead by *great* ideas."[4] Leadership begins with a story[5], a philosophy, a set of core values, a point of view, an educational 'stance' that passionately motivates a leader and engages his or her followers. In previous publications[6], my colleagues and I have carved out our 'story' around a 'great' idea called 'invitational leadership'. An invitation is "a summary description of messages, formal and informal, verbal and non-verbal, continuously transmitted to others to inform them that they are able, worthwhile and responsible."[7] From this definition of an '*invitation*', Louise Stoll and I stated that invitational leadership "is about communicating invitational messages to individuals and groups in order to build and act on a shared and evolving vision of enhanced educational experiences for all pupils."[8] As this definition suggests, and as Chapter 3 will elaborate, our 'story' is not so much a definitive leadership style in competition with academically defined leadership approaches, but rather a values-based approach to leadership and life that promotes life-affirming policies and practices in schools and school districts. Chapter 3, *Values*, therefore develops this 'story' line and encourages leaders of learning to promote learning, teaching and caring in schools by inviting themselves and other personally and professionally.

While there is no magic template for educational leadership, most of us have the capacity to assume an important direct or indirect leadership role in a school or district through the appropriateness of our invitations to others. To do so, we must use all of the intellectual qualities that each of us possesses. While few of us are born leaders, each of us is equipped from birth with a set of intellectual qualities or 'tools' that are vital to leadership. When we walk out the door in the morning, we all carry an intellectual 'tool kit' that serves us throughout life.[9] These tools or qualities include our reason, memory, imagination, intuition, common sense, and ethics. Some 'tools' are well developed, while others are underused. How we develop and use these 'tools' determines our leadership potential. Successful leaders develop and employ all of these qualities in a balanced way to meet the challenges of contemporary leadership. Chapter 4, *Qualities*, addresses each of these tools, describes their power and limitations, and outlines how they connect to the 'learnings' required by 'leaders of learning'.

Like Jane, Allan, Elena, Charmaine and other leaders of learning, we can identify and master a set of crucial 'learnings' that go across time and space and are at the heart of the leadership that promotes student learning.[10] Taken together they provide a conceptual framework for the identification, recruitment, training, selection, and ongoing professional development of school leaders. Recently my colleagues Louise Stoll, Lorna Earl, and myself argued that

> Leadership for learning is not a destination with fixed co-ordinates on a compass, but a journey with plenty of detours and even some dead ends. Effective educational leaders are continuously open to new learning because the journey keeps changing. Their maps are complex and can be confusing. What leaders require for this journey is a set of interrelated 'learnings' looking at school leadership in a holistic rather than reductionist way. These 'learnings' can be deepened, elaborated, nurtured, abandoned, and connected and related to other 'learnings' as the journey progresses.[11]

We suggested seven sets of 'learnings' for leaders of learning that we think go across time and space and apply to all educational leaders. These learnings are:

- understanding learning

- critical thinking

- contextual understanding

- political acumen

- emotional understanding

- making connections

- futures thinking.

Chapter 5, entitled, *Learnings*, develops each of these and connects them to leadership development and succession planning.

Leadership in a school does not rest exclusively on the shoulders of a few formal leaders. Leadership is everywhere. It is like culture; it is intangible, non-rational and non-linear. You see it only in its results. Every person in the school exercises some form of influence over others and directs in some way the daily course of events – from the master teacher mentoring a neophyte, to the staffroom lawyer actively undermining the school's formal leaders. Some informal leaders, for example, have a powerful effect on colleagues, while other formal leaders are mere placeholders with little real influence. Some leaders are part of the school's community of practice, and others are on the periphery or even marginalised by the teaching staff. Wenger[12] tells us that prospective leaders and others follow fairly predictable trajectories to become part of a community of practice whereby they can influence a school's direction. How and in what ways one exercises leadership will depend on a person's trajectory. For example, first year school leaders on an 'inbound trajectory' will have to find ways to move from the periphery of a school's community of practice to an 'insider's trajectory' if they wish to ensure substantive and sustainable changes. Conversely, leaders on an 'outbound trajectory' will have more interest in finding ways to sustain important parts of their legacy. Chapter 6, *Trajectories*, explores the implications of shifting career trajectories for leaders and their leadership, and the different relationships a leader might have with the various 'communities of practice' that exist in a school.

One of my mentors, the late J.W. Singleton, the first Director of the Halton Board of Education[13] in Ontario, Canada, where I worked for twenty three years, was a large man physically and intellectually. A somewhat Churchillian character, he suffered fools badly. A politician at a school board meeting asked him "Mr. Singleton, why do you always promote the best teachers?" He replied, "Madam, would you prefer the alternative?" In many jurisdictions internationally, 'the alternative' is happening. Without well-developed succession management, there is evidence that many schools and school jurisdictions are not attracting high quality school leaders to advertised positions. We know that the best organisations identify, recruit, prepare, select, and support leaders based on their potential, rather than on whether their existing proficiencies fit a job as it exists now.[14] A software company, for example, may know what a software developer does now, but probably doesn't know what a software developer will be doing ten years from now. What they will know, however, is that they want to stay in the software business, so they look for people with the potential to acquire the knowledge, skills and attitudes that will keep them on the cutting edge in a rapidly changing field. We know we will be in the education business in ten to fifteen years but what it will look like is guesswork. What we do know is that we will need educational leaders with the potential to be leaders of learning and the ability to work through others to enhance the learning of all students. Chapter 7, *Succession*, elaborates this argument for succession management and shows how the 'Leadership for Mortals' model can provide a useful way to bring coherence to succession planning as well as to identify and develop the potential of future educational leaders. As a starting point, however, let us turn to the here and now and contextualise this discussion in the present challenges faced by school leaders.

Notes

1   Stoll, L., Fink, D., and Earl, L. (2003). *It's about Learning (and It's about Time)*. London: Routledge/Falmer.

2   Earley, P., Evans, J., Collarbone, P., Gold, A., and Halpin, D. (2002). *Establishing the Current State of School Leadership In England: Research report No. 336*. London: Department for Education and Skills; Williams, T. (2001), *Unrecognized Exodus, Unaccepted Accountability: The looming shortage of principals and vice principals in Ontario public school boards*. Toronto, ON: Ontario Principals Council.

3   Hargreaves, A. (1994). *Changing Teachers, Changing Times*. London: Cassell.

4   Giuliani, R. (2002). *Leadership*. New York: Miramax Books.

5   Gardner, H.(1996). *Leading Minds: An anatomy of leadership*. New York: Basic Books.

6   Stoll, L. and Fink, D. (1996). *Changing Our Schools: Linking school effectiveness and school improvement*. Buckingham: Open University Press.

7   Purkey,W.W. and Novak, J.N. (1984) *Inviting School Success*. 2nd edition, Belmont, CA: Wadsworth.

8   Stoll and Fink, (1996) op.cit. p. 109.

9   Saul, J.R. (2001). *On Equilibrium*. Toronto, ON: Penguin/Viking.

10   Stoll, Fink and Earl (2003). op.cit.

11   Ibid. p.103.

12   Wenger, E. (1998). *Communities of Practice*. Cambridge: Cambridge University Press.

13   The Halton Board of Education, now called the Halton District Board of Education, is located in Ontario Canada

14   See Liebman, M, Bruer R. A., and Maki, B.R. (1996) 'Succession management: The next generation of succession planning', *Human Resource Planning*, 19 (3), pp.16–29; National Academy of Public Administration (1997). *Managing Succession and Developing Leadership: Growing the next generation of public service leaders*. Washington, DC: NAPA; Rothwell, W.J. (2001). *Effective Succession Planning: Ensuring leadership continuity and building talent from within* (2nd edition) New York: AMACOM; Schall, E. (1997). 'Public sector succession: A strategic approach to sustaining innovation, *Public Administration Review*, 57 (1), 4–10; Souque, J.P. (1998). *Succession Planning and Leadership Development*. Ottawa, ON: Conference Board of Canada.

1 *Challenge*

It is symbolic that the first animal that scientists cloned was a sheep – the famous 'Dolly'. Sheep are extremely obedient animals, easily controlled, compliant, and behave in quite predictable ways. A sharp bark from an assertive and single-minded sheep-dog directs the sheep in whatever predetermined direction the dog's owner dictates. The sheep-dog is the ultimate technocrat. It is single-minded, and uncompromising in responding to its master's bidding, methodical, intense, controlling and meticulous in the execution of its duties.

Sadly, the mind of the technocrat appears to drive the current standards/standardisation agenda that has infected educational jurisdictions world wide, and has propagated a type of leadership that is more interested in producing politically attractive test scores than enhancing students' learning. Technocrats choose the technical side of an issue over the social and human consequences and want passionately for reason to crush emotion. Pamela Pitcher[1] has developed a composite picture of the organisational technocrat based on extensive research in an international corporate conglomerate. She produces a portrait of technocrats who value followers like 'Dolly' who never question authority, obediently follow orders and adhere to 'standard operating procedures'. Technocrats always feel the past was simple and their own times more complex so they distrust the experiences of others who do not share their values. They know the management literature better than anyone and can use the rhetoric of decentralisation, empowerment and 'participative management', but rarely decentralise, empower or allow meaningful participation. They are strategic about human relations. Technocrats if they value anyone value other technocrats, so they produce organisational leadership clones, and when things go wrong as they inevitably do, the fault always resides with someone else. The ascendancy of the technocrat in education has paralleled the emergence of New Public

Management (NPM) as the dominant model of policy development in many western educational jurisdictions.[2] By looking at New Public Management in relation to two other policy trends that have dominated the past thirty years we can begin to understand the evolution of different educational leadership approaches.

Traditional Public Administration

Until recent times, those of us who have worked in publicly funded education were part of large, highly centralised organisations such as school districts or Local Education Authorities. Administrators, including school leaders who worked within what might be described as Traditional Public Administration (TPA), were 'rule-driven bureaucrats executing and maintaining norms of integrity ... in a neutral way with the common good in mind. This perspective emphasises reliability, consistency, predictability and accountability'.[3] These bureaucracies focused on the common good of all children and were organised to promote the consistency and reliability of results. Like most educators up until the early 1990s, I spent most of my working life within a traditional management structure.

Central government, in my case the government of Ontario, determined student diploma requirements and teachers' and principals' certification standards, produced curriculum guidelines, and contributed to a greater or lesser extent to the funding of schools. The actual administration of schools fell to a school district directed by a locally elected policy board (Local Education Authority or school district) that through its appointed officials fashioned second generation detailed curriculum documents, hired and fired principals and teachers, allocated resources, and interacted with the district's community. Principals, for example, were accountable to the senior officials above them in the hierarchy and these senior officials were in turn accountable to the elected school board. A major focus for these systems was on equity and a concern for the common good. For the most part, all schools were treated the same. The school district allocated money on a per student formula, paid teachers based on seniority, and assigned principals as determined by the system and an individual school's needs. Where these demands conflicted, system requirements usually prevailed.

Changes tended to be incremental and schools did not stray too far from district procedures. Schools that became too innovative such as model or lighthouse schools usually regressed to the mean in short order.[4] As long as schools and school leaders adhered to approved processes and procedures, the system allowed their leaders considerable leeway in the daily operations of the schools.

While it is dangerous to generalise, educators for the most part saw themselves as public servants who tried to balance the needs of individual students and parents and the collective aspirations of the larger community. For example, as an area superintendent[5] with responsibility for a number of schools, one of my greatest challenges was to administer the school system's optional attendance policy. This policy required students to attend their neighbourhood primary or secondary school for their first year of enrolment. After one year they could move to any other school in the system with no questions asked. The theory behind the policy was that a student or parent could not know a school until the student had at least attended that school. It was believed that only then could they make an informed choice. Once students attended their designated school, we found that they almost invariably stayed. From a system's point of view this policy enabled administrators to balance enrolments so that all schools could offer broad academic, athletic and arts programs for all students, not just programs for an elite.

It was the job of the area superintendent to adjudicate parental appeals for exemption from this policy. My colleagues and I tried to weigh parental needs against those of the school and the total student population. I would on occasion get a parental request for a son or daughter to attend a non-designated school that, according to the parent, had a 'better class of students' – which could be translated as, 'I want my child in a school without students from minority backgrounds'. If I had acceded I would have created a stampede of 'white flight'. From my point of view a negative decision in a case of this nature was rather easy, but many situations were not so straightforward. One of my upper-middle-class schools offered Latin as an option. A number of parents used this as a reason to get their son or daughter into the more socially prestigious school. It was much harder to decide whether the student really wanted to take Latin or whether this was a ruse to 'beat the system'. I suspect in this age of 'the customer is always right' that my example sounds like bureaucratic interference, but the rights and opportunities of all the students and their parents seemed to me to be a more defensible and more ethical operating principle. As slow-moving and rule-bound as school systems might have been within TPA, there was a genuine attempt to attend to the needs of all parents and students, not just the affluent, the knowledgeable, the pushy, or the influential.

While these bureaucracies may have moved slowly, they did change, especially as regards the role of leaders. In my early years in education as I worked my way up the hierarchy, school districts tended to look for leadership candidates with strong managerial skills, especially at the secondary level where school leaders had to construct timetables. In the 1970s as the politics of education became more turbulent, the school districts expected their administrators to possess not only managerial and organisational skills but also people and political skills. The pervasiveness of the school effectiveness and school improvement movements in the 1980s meant that leaders now must also have expertise in teaching and learning. The term 'instructional leader' became current, and school systems expected their leaders to assume this mantle. In my own school system an effective schools project[6] and the University of Toronto Learning Consortium[7], among other professional enriching programs[8], involved leaders in supporting each other by addressing ways to enhance students' learning. Like many school districts in Ontario in the 1980s, this focus on student learning was beginning to provide significant payoff.[9] By the mid-1990s, however, these innovative and professionally enriching activities came to a screeching halt, as school jurisdictions turned to New Public Management (NPM) as a way to energise purportedly moribund educational systems.

New Public Management

Born during the Thatcher years in Britain and the Reagan years in the United States, New Public Management promised to usher in a new era of low-cost educational reform, and a remedy for the long-held belief that TPA was ineffective and too slow-moving to respond to the pressures of a globalised economy and the shrinking of time and space through technology. While few would argue with this appraisal of TPA, the solutions offered by NPM, were to say the least, problematic. The renowned management expert Henry Mintzberg[10] has described NPM as merely a new label for "old corporate values". Government he adds 'is not business; treating it as such demeans it. As for treating us like customers, I expect a lot more from my government than that, thank you. I am a citizen, not a mere customer.' NPM in education promised significant improvements in educational results while offering dramatic savings in taxes through market driven accountability. It was argued that competitive business markets successfully produced excellent, low-priced products, therefore, why not apply this market technology to education? Similarly, governments adopted the prevailing business philosophy that advocated decentralisation of decision making based on the premise that the best decisions are made at the level in the organisation where the decisions have to be carried out; budgets should be devolved to schools through site-based management (or local management of schools in the UK).[11]

The final cornerstone of NPM in education was community involvement. To this end, some jurisdictions, like New Zealand and New Brunswick in Canada, totally eliminated school districts (LEAs) or, as in the cases of the United Kingdom and Ontario, reduced their powers drastically and devolved considerable responsibilities previously held by school districts and their administrators to councils of locally elected (or appointed) school governors. Some of these local councils, such as school governors in the case of the UK, have the power to hire and fire, reward and discipline principals (school heads)[12] and teachers and can wield considerable influence on daily operations within schools. While the rhetoric of these moves has focused on local democracy, a more cynical view is that the elimination of school districts removes a strong political impediment to a central government's agenda. How democratic these local councils are is also a matter of dispute. As Mortimore and his colleagues found in their study of British primary schools, local elites of more affluent parents often dominate these local councils and create divisions in the school community between 'insiders' and 'outsiders'.[13] For school leaders and particularly principals, this move has required them to develop or polish their political skills and spend more time in 'the care and feeding' of local politicians and less time attending to teaching and learning in their schools.

As NPM became the policy process of choice, governments across the western world initiated a wave of reform in the late 1980s and well into the 1990s. Educational jurisdictions engaged in a race to impose a new educational orthodoxy[14] on their schools that demanded new and tough curriculum standards for students to ensure that these nations, states and provinces were economically competitive in the globalised economy. Lurking behind this agenda was a distrust of educational professionals in general and their unions in particular, and a view that any opposition to or criticism of this 'orthodoxy' was the work of self-serving interest groups.

While few people would oppose the goal of improved educational achievement, in reality these standards have tended to become standardised into national, state or provincial curricula, supported by standardised tests to ensure accountability and customer information to help 'consumers' make informed choices about schools, and including increasingly standardised teaching strategies or 'best practices'. This very rational, linear and technocratic approach to educational change has run into one fundamental roadblock however – the students are non-standard, and teaching and leading are often non-rational activities. As a colleague once proclaimed, "the parents keep sending the wrong kids." Not only do students' needs, interests, abilities, learning styles and learning rates differ, but also so do their genders, ethnicities, religions, first languages, and cultures. Somehow, teaching to 'Norm', that mythical student who sits firmly in the middle of the class and achieves better that half of his classmates and not as well as the other half, is no longer appropriate.

Related closely to this standard's paradox is a push for 'deep learning', learning for understanding – undoubtedly an admirable goal.[15] Like the focus on high standards, 'the devil is in the details'. Let us suppose a jurisdiction needs a new curriculum for the middle years (ages 11 to 13). Most jurisdictions design curriculum by committee and send specialists off to different settings to decide what students in the example of the middle years should learn. Since these committee members are specialists who are steeped in their subjects and look at the world through their unique prisms, they design with their particular passions and prejudices in mind. This results in courses of study that when aggregated are so 'stuffed' with content that students are subjected to a 'hurried' curriculum that does not provide the time for students and teachers to explore topics in depth. To compound the problem, schools organise these various subjects into neat little packages of time for all subjects, regardless of what amount of learning is required in each, and then at the end of the day schools expect students to integrate their learning. I have worked with committees containing some outstanding subject experts who have found the challenge of integrating curriculum very, very, difficult, yet schools expect students to do what the professionals find quite complex. In turn, teachers challenged by their need to cover the curriculum to ensure students are ready for high stakes tests race through the mandated curriculum with little time to contextualise "students' learning in what they have learned before, in what other teachers are also teaching them, and in students' own cultures and lives."[16]

A related but no less 'unintended consequence' of the new 'educational orthodoxy' produced by NPM is a contraction of the curriculum for the most challenged and marginalised students. School jurisdictions have logically zeroed in on literacy and numeracy as key building blocks for future learning. For example, the British government has poured millions of pounds into its literacy and numeracy strategies. Similarly, the Bush government's No Child Left Behind policy in the USA has attacked issues of literacy and numeracy through more testing of students, accountability for teachers, and a reward and punishment strategy for a school's performance. The high stakes nature and political profile of both of these strategies, however, has forced teachers to focus on short-term literacy and numeracy goals for their most challenged students, and in the process has narrowed the curriculum for students who probably need such subjects as the arts, vocational programs and physical education as much, if not more, than more advantaged students. It seems paradoxical that the most needy students get the most sterile curriculum. As Bracy[17] states in his report on American education in 2004,

> far too many news stories this year began with sentences like this "To give her third graders an extra 50 minutes of reading daily, the principal has eliminated music, art, and gym." "Raymond Middle School lost its two art teachers last year. Home economics was eliminated along with most foreign language classes and some physical education classes."

NPM also valorises neutral measurement of educational efficacy, usually expressed in terms of numbers. If in business the shareholders can keep score of their investments, then the educational share-holders, the taxpayers, should be able to determine just as easily how well their educational investments are paying off. This simple logic has appeal, but determining the payoff on educational invest-ments is long term and not easily defined and measured in the short term like quarterly profits. This is not a defence of the status quo. Most educators want to be held accountable, but they don't want to be held responsible for things over which they have no control such as poverty, inadequate budgets, run down school buildings, and transient students. They also recognise the importance of assess-ment in promoting student learning, but not just the assessment *of* learning but more importantly 'assessment *for* learning' and assess-ment *as* learning.[18] Recently educational scholars have corroborated what good teachers have always known and called for a paradigm shift that focuses educational assessment on 'supporting learning rather than on sorting and selecting students'. They argue that most educational measurement specialists still operate from a dated behaviourist perspective with little consideration of contemporary theories of learning and cognition.[19] If educators are to be held truly accountable for teaching and learning then the indicators of their efforts must be more sensitive to the nuances of teaching and learn-ing and the non-standardised nature of the students they teach, rather than the obsolete, blunt but inexpensive instruments that allegedly measure students' learning at that moment.

In line with the demand for accountability that is inherent in NPM and the need for a 'bottom line' that is simple and easily inter-preted, governments internationally have blitzed schools with stan-dardised tests. Standardised tests can provide excellent information on the strengths and weaknesses of a curriculum, help schools address general programming issues, and if used effectively by teach-ers, inform instructional decisions. The overuse of assessments in many jurisdictions however is approaching a 'pathology of inten-sity'.[20] This occurs when society takes something that is useful, and overuses it to the point that it becomes ineffectual, such as peni-cillin in the treatment of SARS and some forms of syphilis. High stakes assessments *of* learning have become so numerous and perva-sive that their effects have become increasingly short term and anti-thetical to sustainable long-term changes.[21] The international obsession with assessment *of* learning undermines the intellectual growth of students because it consumes an inordinate amount of time in checking for growth that could be used for supporting growth – 'deep' learning and assessment *for* learning.

My grandsons have both recently participated in the Educational Quality Assurance Office's (EQAO) large scale testing for grade 3 and grade 6 in the province of Ontario.[22] For both boys and for many like them, capable middle-class students, it was a non-event. For most of their teachers in the leafy suburb in which they live, it was an inconvenience. For teachers in a nearby inner city, however, where poverty is endemic and special education needs under-served, it was an ordeal and a threat. On most standardised tests or assessments such as those set by the EQAO, one third of the students are like my grandsons and will pass without difficulty, one third will fail and learn early in life that they are failures – which leaves the one third that can go one way or the other. So the argument is about how do we boost this middle third to make a school look good? In Ontario, EQAO only interrupts two weeks of the children's learning. In some places, however, there is so much time given over to preparing for tests and then writing them up, that I wonder when students have enough time to learn something more important than becoming a good test taker.[23] If life required the skills necessary to perform on most multiple-choice or recall tests then the investment of time, energy and money that goes into standardised testing might be worthwhile. But the last time I looked, the world was a pretty complex place and students need rather sophisticated problem-solving skills.

Government pressure on school leaders to make this flawed system work forces them to attempt to motivate reluctant teachers to work harder and achieve more in a climate of politically biased, systemic, cleverly orchestrated criticism and humiliation in many educational jurisdictions. For example, without any verifiable evidence a former Chief Inspector of Schools for England and Wales glibly announced that the country had 15,000 incompetent teachers. This number proved to be wonderful fodder for the right wing press, and only served to make the job of school leaders much more difficult.[24] In Ontario from 1995 until 2003, a Progressive Conservative government took every opportunity to criticise teachers and their unions. The province's Minister of Education declared to his officials that we must 'create a crisis' by exaggerating the problems of the school system in Ontario as a way to promote the government's agenda. In this climate, public officials entreated leaders in the brave new world of NPM to become 'instructional leaders'. Leadership was seen as something that people with formal power do to people without it. The role of leaders was to attend to "the behaviours of teachers as they engage in activities directly affecting the growth of students."[25] Heroically, the leader, usually narrowly defined as the principal (or school head), had to know how each teacher was teaching and how to help each one to teach more effectively. Effectiveness, however, has many meanings depending on context. Some educational divisions, particularly in the USA, define effectiveness almost exclusively in terms of how well students achieve on standardised tests. England determines effectiveness through a combination of external testing and central government inspections that determine effectiveness based on a government template of efficiency, effectiveness and economy. With little discretionary time and a need to respond to external pressures, 'instructional leadership' for many principals means using various appraisal systems, including performance pay in some places, to pressure teachers into ratcheting up student performance as determined by high-stakes tests.

Ironically, within the technocratic world of New Public Management, governments have centralised the very 'stuff' of education – the 'what', 'when', and 'how do we know' – and downloaded budgets, repairing toilets, hiring and firing custodial staff, and organising transportation routes to the schools and their leaders in the name of site-based management. With the demise of intermediary agencies such as schools districts and Local Education Authorities that often performed these tasks under TPA, school leaders have assumed responsibility for all of the related management and administration of their establishments. Many school leaders have willingly bought into this model because it is a great deal easier to arrange for a new roof than to work with the mediocre teacher who is just good enough to avoid being fired but not good enough to truly inspire students' learning. Besides, that new roof is a visible symbol of a leader's legacy, but the modest improvement of the mediocre teacher is often very difficult to display and extremely hard and frustrating work. It is more rewarding and much easier to manage things than to be an 'instructional leader' or a 'leader of learning'.

School leaders within NPM must not only be managers who can ensure the smooth operation of their schools, they must also become excellent marketers of their schools, facilitators of quality teachers' lessons, agents for improved student outcomes, and sophisticated politicians who can work effectively with empowered local councils. School leadership has become 'greedy' work because organisations now make "total claims on their members and attempt to encompass within their circle the whole personality."[26] This view of leadership is enshrined in numerous policy documents in many educational jurisdictions that list the competencies or 'standards' for school leaders.

Best practice: a technocrat's dream

Around the world there appears to be a search for a 'Holy Grail' of 'best practice' in leadership: what I described elsewhere as a technocrat's dream.[27] My attribution is that technocrats create lists of 'best practices' to emphasise the technical conceptions of a problem or activity to avoid addressing the human and social consequences of their policies, and use these lists as benchmarks for the recruitment and assessment of 'designer' leaders.[28] For example, Ken Leithwood and his colleagues from the University of Toronto surveyed leadership standards from Australia, New Zealand, the UK, and the USA and listed 121 leadership practices that are necessary for leaders to succeed in the contemporary policy environment.[29] The 'lists' or 'templates' that do exist seem to require people of heroic abilities to lead schools. Principals are not only required to lead, manage and attend to culture along with structure;[30] they must unite their school through "inspiring visions"[31] that empower others by "distributing" leadership among colleagues.[32] This pressure has led to feelings of "overwhelming responsibilities, information perplexity, and emotional anxiety."[33] New principals are described as "frightened" by the challenge of principalship.[34] Since most of us are merely mortal, such lists simply promote guilt (at not being able to achieve everything on the list), martyrdom (from trying to do everything) or the compliant messenger ("I'm just doing what they tell us to do" – the Albert Speer defence). Paradoxically, at a time when policy makers place so much importance on leadership, it would appear that many reform policies actually inhibit leadership and oblige school principals and other educational leaders to become little more than the managers of externally mandated changes. As a beleaguered principal in the *Change Over Time* study exclaimed, "sometimes the rules change, day by day in terms of what we can and can't do." He added, "no sooner are we … moving forward in the direction that we believed we need to go, other changes and outside pressures have been imposed on us as well. So things that you want to do have to take a back seat sometimes and that can be quite frustrating."[35]

As a result, leadership succession has become an increasingly urgent issue in many western educational jurisdictions in recent years as the aging 'baby boom' generation moves on.[36] Equally worrying is the growing disenchantment of many potential leaders with the changing nature of leadership roles as a result of the standards/standardisation agenda.[37] One of the Ontario principals in the *Change Over Time* project, a woman in her early forties engaged in her first principalship, expressed her frustration with the pressures to ensure that her school complies with government reforms when she declared, "I feel like I am responsible for the whole world". There is increasing evidence that she is not alone.[38] In the USA, the National Association of Secondary School Principals (2001) reported that the average age of principals in 1993–94 was 47.7, with 37.0 per cent over age 50, 53.6 per cent between ages 40 and 49, and 9.5 per cent age 39 or under. Half of the school districts surveyed in 2000 reported that there was a shortage of qualified candidates. "This shortage occurred among rural schools (52 per cent), suburban schools (45 per cent), and urban schools (47 per cent). These shortages of qualified principal candidates also occurred at all levels: elementary (47 per cent), junior high/middle (55 per cent), and senior high (55 per cent)".[39] The NASSP attributes this failure to attract quality leaders to:

> increased job stress, inadequate school funding, balancing school management with instructional leadership, new curriculum standards, educating an increasingly diverse student population, shouldering responsibility that once belonged at home or in the community, and then facing possible termination if their schools don't show instant results.[40]

A similar pattern exists in Canada and particularly in Ontario. A study by the Ontario Principals Council (OPC) shows that close to 60 per cent of principals and 30 per cent of assistant principals in elementary and secondary schools in public school boards will retire by 2005. By 2010, more than 80 per cent of principals and about 50 per cent of assistant principals will retire. The study forecasts that 1,900 Ontario schools out of about 3,200 in the English component of the public system will have a new principal by 2004. Moreover, the study reports that close to 8,000 teachers with principal and assistant principal qualifications are likely to retire by 2005, while only 715 teachers on average have acquired principal qualifications each year between 1997 and 2000.[41] In England, 45 per cent of the 25,000 school heads (principals) are over 50 and will retire before 2014.[42]

Love it or loathe it, New Public Management has profoundly affected the working lives of principals, teachers, and other educators. In particular it has changed the focus on 'inputs and processes' under TPA to 'outcomes and results'. This is a significant paradigm shift for educators. I have sat on both sides of the bargaining table during teacher contract talks. In addition to money, the conversations invariably focused on class sizes and pupil–teacher contacts. The argument I made as a union agent and that I heard as part of a management team was "we can do a much better job if we just had fewer students in our classes". It seems to me that optimum class size was always five students fewer than existed at any given moment. When we had 40 students in our classes we used to say, we could do a really good job with only 35. Since teachers' unions could offer little proof of improved student achievement they had to rely on the logic of their argument and trust in the profession. Unfortunately, for whatever reasons, the logic failed to convince and society stopped trusting and began to demand observable, measurable results. Education is at a crossroads. TPA is dated and obsolete and NPM has failed to deliver on its promises, and now many governments internationally are pouring resources into state education in an attempt to resuscitate bruised and battered educational systems.

The learning community

Added to the mix in recent years, are the scholars and business gurus who have begun to talk about another approach to organisational management and public policy development which is called 'organisational learning'. Popularised by Peter Senge[43] in the early 1990s, organisational learning (OL) recognises the turbulence of our times, and the need for organisations to build their internal capacity to respond to an unknowable future. Definitions of organisational learning range from organisations in which the individual can learn, to organisations in which people learn together as a team. Mulford has synthesised the literature of organisational learning in schools and identified four attributes of schools in which OL is operative – a trusting and collaborative culture, a shared and monitored mission, a risk taking climate and on-going and relevant professional development.[44] Increasingly scholars have extended OL to develop a rich body of educational literature[45] on 'Learning Communities' that has incorporated and expanded the idea of organisational learning to encompass the many stakeholders involved in education. The idea of a learning community (LC) includes not just the professionals but also parents, students and the community at large in dialogue and shared learning about the purposes, practices and policies of a school and a school district.

My colleagues and I described six processes that not only help define the idea of a Learning Community but also operationalise it.[46]

1 *Community dialogue* refers to what Senge describes as "the capacity of members of a team to suspend assumptions and enter into a genuine 'thinking together' … allowing the group to discover insights not attainable individually."[47] It is through dialogue with all stakeholders that schools and districts arrive at a shared sense of meaning which is crucial to their ability to respond to changing contexts.

2 *Self-evaluation* involves the entire school or district community keeping the organisation under review. Results of assessments and inspections should not be a surprise. The organisation uses whatever data and evidence available, to both problem solve and problem seek.

3 *Team Learning* provides opportunities for groups of professionals and other involved partners in education to engage in the planning of a school or district's immediate and long-range goals and policies. Such teams can be as few as two teachers planning a unit for seven year olds on a cross-curricular topic, to a secondary school history department of eight teachers developing a

theme on historical causation, to a school-wide team of 20 teachers, parents and students developing cross-curricular approaches to 'assessment for learning', to a district-wide committee determining that district's goals for the ensuing years. Great teams in schools are like great athletic teams or musical groups or political campaign teams. As some coaches are fond of saying, and it is true 'there is no "I" in team' – individuals sacrifice their personal goals and aspirations for the good of the team and its purposes. They focus on the team's goals, participate openly and honestly in team dialogue, share leadership, and address conflict in ways that focus on ideas not personalities.

4   *Reculturing* addresses the cultural aspects of an organisation. Culture has many meanings, some complex, but I prefer the simple. Culture is "the way we do things around here"[48] or Gareth Morgan's, "How organisations work when no-one is looking."[49] Culture is a "way of life."[50] It defines reality for those who work in a social organisation; it also provides support, identity and "forms a framework for occupational learning."[51] Within schools cultural norms are those rules not written down in any staff or student handbook, but rather they are the mutually understood standards for daily living. You usually learn the rules by inadvertently breaking them.

Elsewhere my colleague Louise Stoll and I have identified ten cultural norms for improving schools that have the capacity to deal with change. We have added an explanatory catchphrase that elaborates the meaning of each norm.

- Shared goals – 'we know where we're going'

- Responsibility for success – 'we can succeed'

- Collegiality – 'we're working on this together'

- Continuous improvement – 'we can get better'

- Lifelong learning – 'learning is for everyone'

- Risk taking – 'we learn by trying something new'

- Support – 'there's always someone there to help'

- Mutual respect – 'everyone has something to offer'

- Openness – 'we can discuss our differences'

- Celebration and humour – 'we feel good about ourselves'[52]

Learning communities continually revisit and challenge the cultural norms of the school in such a way as to make the invisible visible, and the unspoken spoken, to bring the school's 'communities of practice'[53] into line with the cultural norms of a learning community.

5   *Creativity and spontaneity* based on trust and strong interpersonal relationships provide the energy for learning communities. Openness to experience and learning drives these communities to imagine the unimaginable and try the impossible. Gary Hamel explains that in the business world "companies fail to create the future not because they fail to predict it, but because they fail to imagine it. It is creativity and curiosity that they lack, not perspicuity."[54] In the modern world, experimentation is the key to progress. Tom Peters, an American business writer, advises organisations to "fail, forward, fast." He explains, "If nothing goes awry, then nothing new can emerge. That is an iron law of nature."[55] Learning communities do not fear failure. In fact they embrace it as a learning experience, and a building block for future greatness.

6   *Making connections* is the ability to see 'the big picture'. It is also described as 'systems thinking' or 'joined up thinking'. It's about looking at the forest, not just the trees. It is about seeing interconnections and interrelationships within an organisation. It is essential to understand how the school as a whole and its parts relate to each other, and how it connects to its community, district and beyond. A useful metaphor is to think of a school or a school system as similar to the child's activity of connecting the dots. Young children are often asked to connect dot 1 to dot 2 to dot 3 and so on, and by the end of this activity they have sketched the outline of a picture which they are usually asked to colour in. Schools and systems are made up of a myriad of dots, and the ability to connect them to create large understandable pictures contributes significantly to their success as learning

communities. How we connect one teacher to another, or one department to another, or the school to the community, or the math curriculum to the science curriculum, or how we create a school-wide strategy for student problem solving are just a few of the countless networked connections that learning communities must make.

Conclusion

Many years ago a riotous song called *Jake the Peg* by the Australian entertainer, Rolf Harris, became internationally popular. 'Jake' was a three-legged man who found difficulty knowing which leg to use at any given moment and inevitably fell on his face. Leaders in the first decade of the twenty first century are like 'Jake the Peg', the three-legged man. They have one leg in Traditional Public Administration since most still work in hierachial bureaucracies, one leg in New Public Management as they struggle with state curricula, standardised tests, and site-based management, and a third leg in Learning Communities as they work to refocus their schools and communities on students' learning. The challenge for a leader in education is to learn how to balance on all three legs while simultaneously leading their school to become a learning community.

Technocratic leaders are insufficiently flexible and dextrous to meet this challenge. In an environment that values predictability, control and compliance, technocrats have their place, but that place isn't to be in charge of building organisational capacity or promoting the kinds of educational change that will be necessary to prepare our students for a knowledge society. The challenge of 'the three-legged man' is beyond the capabilities of any one person, regardless of how heroic, charismatic or brilliant he or she may be. Rather than looking at school leaders as individuals, we need to look at school leadership as a pervasive force across schools and school districts, and how dedicated 'mortals' can blend together to shape this school and district leadership in ways that ensure challenging and creative learning experiences for all students. It is in this direction that the remainder of the book is heading.

Notes

1   Pitcher, P. (1997). *Artists, Craftsmen and Technocrats*. Toronto: John Wiley.

2   I base this discussion on Bill Mulford's comprehensive (2003) study of public policy and its effect on leadership, 'School leaders: Changing roles and impact on teacher and school effectiveness: A paper commissioned by the Education and Training Policy Division', in Organisation for Economic Cooperation and Development (OECD), pp. 1–65.

3   Olson, J. (2002). 'Towards a European administrative space? Advanced research on the Europeanisation of the nation-state' (ARENA). University of Oslo: working paper, No.26.

4   See Fink, D. (2000). *Good Schools, Real Schools: Why school reform doesn't last*. New York: Teachers' College Press.

5   This position is comparable to a local 'inspector' of a group of schools.

6   Stoll, L. and Fink, D. (1996). *Changing Our Schools: Linking school effectiveness and school improvement*. Buckingham, UK: Open University Press.

7   The Learning Consortium was a professional development network among four large Toronto area school boards, the University of Toronto, and the Ontario Institute for Studies in Education. It extended the idea of links between university faculties of education and schools beyond a small number of innovative, showcase or professional development schools to entire school systems. The Consortium promoted a powerful, wide-ranging strategy to integrate pre-service teacher education, teacher induction, on-going professional development, and whole-school change.

8   Fink, D. and Stoll, L. (1997). 'Weaving school and teacher development together', in T. Townsend (ed.), *Restructuring and Quality*. London: Routledge.

9   When the Halton school district replicated the Second International Mathematics Study (TIMSS), its students far surpassed national and international norms at all levels. Part of this is explainable by the district's socio-economic status, but another part of this can be traced to the emphasis on learning at the school and district levels.

10 Mintzberg, H. (2004). *Managers not MBAs: A hard look at the soft practice of managing and management development*. San Francisco, CA: Berrett-Koehler Publishers , p. 158.

11 For a fuller discussion of the rationale for site-based management, see Caldwell, B.J. and Hayward, D.K. (1998) *The Future of Schools*, London: Falmer; Caldwell, B.J. and Spinks, J.M. (1998) *Beyond the Self-Managing School*, London: Falmer; Caldwell, B.J. and Spinks,

J.M. (1992) *Leading the Self-Managing School*, London: Falmer; Caldwell, B.J. and Spinks, J.M. (1988) *The Self-Managing School*, London: Falmer. For a critique of site-based management see Bishop, P. and Mulford, B. (1996). 'Empowerment in four primary schools: They don't really care'. *International Journal of Educational Reform*, 5 (2): pp. 193–204; Leithwood, K., Jantzi, D. and Steinback, R. (2002). 'School leadership and the new right', in K. Leithwood, P. Hallinger, P. Furman, P. Gronn, J. MacBeath, B. Mulford and K. Riley (eds), *Second International Handbook of Educational Leadership and Administration*. Norwell, MA: Kluwer.

12 For consistency I will use the term 'principal' for a school head, 'assistant principal' for deputy head or vice-principal.

13 Mortimore, P., Sammons, P., Stoll, L., Lewis, D. and Ecob, R. (1988). *School Matters: The junior years*. Buckingham, UK: Open University Press.

14 See Hargreaves, A., Earl, L., Moore, S. and Manning, S. (2001). *Learning to Change: Teaching subjects beyond subjects and standards*. San Francisco, CA: Jossey-Bass, for a detailed discussion of the new educational orthodoxy and its implications.

15 See Hargreaves, A. and Fink, D. (2004). 'The seven principles of sustainable leadership'. *Educational Leadership*, 61 (7): pp. 8–13, and Hargreaves, A. and Fink, D. (2003), 'Sustaining leadership', *Phi Delta Kappa*, 84 (9): pp. 693–700, and Hargreaves, A. and Fink, D. (2005), *Sustainable Leadership*. San Francisco, CA: Jossey-Bass, for a further discussion of 'deep learning' and its importance.

16 Hargreaves, A. and Fink, D. (2000) ibid., p. 30.

17 Bracy, G. (2004). 'The condition of public education: The 14th Bracey report', *Phi Delta Kappa*, 86 (2): 149–66.

18 Earl, L. (2003). *Assessment as Learning: Using classroom assessment to maximize student learning*. Thousand Oaks, CA: Corwin.

19 Delandshere, G. (2004). 'Assessment as inquiry', *Teachers' College Record*, at www.tcrecord.org, p.1.

20 Homer-Dixon, T. (2000). *The Ingenuity Gap: Can we solve the problems of the future?* Toronto, ON: Alfred A. Knopf, p. 175.

21 See Hargreaves and Fink (2005; 2004; 2003) op.cit., for an elaboration of this perspective.

22 EQAO, uses testing as a teaching–learning vehicle in reading, writing and mathematics.

23 Meek, C. (2003). 'Classroom crisis: It's about time', *Phi Delta Kappa*, 84 (8): pp: 592–95; Stoll, L., Fink, D. and Earl, L. (2002). *It's About Learning (and It's About Time)*. London: Routledge/Falmer.

24 The effects of the 'naming, shaming' policy in Britain were devastating. I have conducted workshops with thousands of British educators and I can attest to the discouragement in the face of official condemnations.

25 Leithwood, K., Jantzi, D. and Steinbach, R. (1999). *Changing Leadership for Changing Times*. Buckingham, UK: Open University Press.

26 Gronn, P. (2003) *The New Work of Educational Leaders: Changing leadership practice in an era of school reform*. London: Paul Chapman Publishing, p. 148.

27 Fink, D. (2005). 'Preparing leaders for their future not our past'. In M. Coles and G. Southworth (eds), *Developing Leadership: Creating the schools of tomorrow*. Maidenhead, UK: Open University Press, pp. 1–21.

28 Gronn, P. (2003) op. cit. p. 8.

29 Leithwood et al. (2002) op. cit.

30 Davidson, B.M. and Taylor, D.L. (1999). 'The effects of principal succession in an accelerated school', paper presented at the annual meeting of the American Educational Research Association. San Diego, CA, April 13–17.

31 Takahashi, S.S. (1998). 'The keeper of the house: Principal succession and the mending of the hearts', paper presented at the annual meeting of the American Educational Research Association. San Diego, CA, April 13–17.

32 See Elmore, R. F. (2000). *Building a New Structure for School Leadership*. Washington, D.C.: Albert Shanker Institute; Supovitz, J.A. (2000). 'Manage less: Lead more', in *Principal Leadership*, 1 (3): pp. 14–19; Blase, J. and Blase, J. (1999). 'Shared governance principals: The inner experience', *NASSP Bulletin*, 83 (606): 81–93.

33 Whitaker, K.S. (1999). 'Principal role changes and implications for principalship candidates', *International Journal of Educational Reform*, 8 (4): 352–62.

34 Mansell, N. (2002). 'New heads frightened by top job', *Times Educational Supplement*, 13 September, p. 7.

35 Fink, D. (2003). 'Stewart Heights: From village school to cultural mosaic', in A. Hargreaves and I. Goodsen (eds), *Change Over Time Study*. Spencer Foundation, Major Grant Number: 199800214, p. 41.

36 I develop this further in Chapters 6 and 7.

37 See Earley, P., Evans, J., Collarbone, P., Gold, A. and Halpin, D. (2002). *Establishing the Current State of School Leadership In England: Research report No. 336*. London: Department for Education and Skills; Williams, T. (2001) *Unrecognized Exodus, Unaccepted Accountability: The looming shortage of principals and vice principals in Ontario public school boards*. Toronto: Ontario Principals Council; Murphy, J. (1994) 'Transformational change and the evolving role of the school principal', in J. Murphy and K. Seashore-Louis (eds), *Reshaping the Principalship: Insights from Transformational Reform Efforts*. Thousand Oaks, CA: Corwin

38 See Gronn, P. (2003) op. cit., and Young, M.D. and McLeod, S. (2001). 'Flukes, opportunities and planned interventions: Factors

affecting women's decisions to become school administrators', *Educational Administration Quarterly*, 37 (4): pp. 462–501.

39   Quinn, T. (2002). 'Succession Planning: Start today', National Association of Secondary Principals website, at www.nassp.org.

40   National Association of Secondary School Principals (2001). Press Release: The Principal Shortage. Reston, VA: NASSP, p. 1.

41   Williams (2001) op. cit.

42   Paton, G. (2004). 'Who will replace the ageing heads?', *Times Educational Supplement*, 19 November, p. 2.

43   Senge, P.M. (1990). *The Fifth Discipline: The art and practice of the learning organization.* London: Century Business.

44   Mulford, B. (2002). 'The global challenge: A matter of balance', *Educational Management and Administration*, 30 (2): pp. 123–38.

45   See Louis, K.S-. and Marks, H. (1998) 'Does professional community affect the classroom? Teachers' work and student experiences in restructured schools', *American Journal of Education*, 106 (40): pp. 532–75; MacGilchrist, B., Myers, K. and Reed, J. (1997) *The Intelligent School.* London: Paul Chapman Publishing; Mitchell, C. and Sackney, L. (1998) 'Learning about organizational learning', in K. Leithwood and K.S-. Louis (eds), *Organizational Learning in Schools.* Lisse, the Netherlands: Swets & Zeitlinger; Mitchell, C. and Sackney, L. (2000) *Profound Improvement: Building capacity for a learning community.* Lisse, the Netherlands: Swets & Zeitlinger.

46   Stoll, Fink And Earl (2002) op. cit.

47   Senge, P.M. (1990) op. cit., p. 243.

48   Deal, T.E. and Kennedy, A. (1983). 'Culture and school performance', *Educational Leadership*, 40 (5): pp. 140–41.

49   Morgan, G. (1997). *Images of Organization.* Thousand Oaks, CA, and London: Sage.

50   Hargreaves, D.H. (1995). 'School culture, school effectiveness and school improvement', *School Effectiveness and School Improvement*, 6 (1): pp. 23–46.

51   Hargreaves, A. (1994). *Changing Teachers, Changing Times.* London: Cassell, p. 165.

52   Stoll and Fink, op. cit. For the norms of a 'cruising' school see Stoll, L. and Fink, D. (1997). 'The cruising school: The unidentified ineffective school'. In L. Stoll and K. Myers (eds), *Schools in Difficulty: No quick fixes.* Chichester: Falmer Press.

53   Wenger, E. (1998). *Communities of Practice.* Cambridge: Cambridge University Press.

54   Hamel, G. (2003). 'Be your own seer', in *Business Leadership: A Jossey-Bass reader.* San Francisco, CA: Jossey-Bass, p. 406.

55   Peters, T. (2003). *Re-imagine! Business excellence in a disruptive age.* New York: DK Publishing, p. 27.

2   *Commitment*

I would like you to meet Wayne and Garry. Wayne was the principal of Lord Byron High School when I joined the staff of this innovative school in 1970. Garry was his assistant principal. This was the first year for each in their respective roles. Wayne was a visionary who had an image of a school that responded to the individual needs, interests and abilities of its students, as opposed to the traditional school of the time that forced all students to fit into pre-existing structures. A former colleague who was renowned for her intolerance of pretence described Wayne this way.

> I am not a hero worshipper but when I look back, he had a quiet leadership style rather than a really aggressive one, but I think his encouragement made people want to follow. In fact, he tended to make leaders rather than followers. He would ask pertinent questions and lead you down the path to start something new ... he assumed you would do a top-notch job and you did. You tended to live up to expectations.

One school document described his vision for the school like this,

> Our aspirations for Lord Byron are the development of a humane educational environment for students: a situation in which conduct and growth will develop from *reason* and *mutual respect* and *trust*. Only through an appreciation of these basic and individual needs can we achieve an educational experience which will enable students to realize their optimum potential. This experience, it is hoped, will be characterized by an atmosphere of continuous self-evaluation and improvement.[1]

It must be remembered that this was written long before governments had thought about 'personalised' learning,[2] and long before school improvement and self-evaluation had become pervasive parts of the educational landscape.

In its comment on leadership in the 1975 evaluation of Lord Byron, an external committee of high-ranking government officials from across the province of Ontario declared:

> As well as observing those in formal positions (principal, assistant principals, department chairs) exercise enlightened leadership, we noted that teachers are able to contribute significantly to the decision-making process, not only within the departmental structure. The administration has consciously provided opportunities for recognition of leadership among staff, other than those formally designated as chairmen. This approach has not only guaranteed high quality leadership within the school, but has served as a training ground for an exceptional number of persons who have moved on to positions of leadership within the system.[3]

The report concluded its discussion of leadership by commending the school "for its effective leadership development program."[4] Clearly, Wayne was a 'leader of leaders' and what Pamela Pitcher[5] would call an 'artist'.

Artists

From her research Pitcher identifies three archetypes, the 'technocrat' described in the last chapter, the 'artist', and the 'craftsman'. Pitcher portrays the founder of the multinational corporation that she studied as a man with high emotional intelligence, who had a vision of building a medium-sized company into a company that spanned the globe. His audacious plan was to marry general and life insurance, banking, trust and investments services, at a time when most people believed banking and insurance were incompatible. After fifteen years, the company was worth $20 billion and was an integrated service company in Europe, Asia and North America. His colleagues described him as a warm, generous, people-oriented, imaginative, daring, and funny person. Pitcher explains these attributes helped him to attract and keep great colleagues and investors. He shared the glory and the rewards and made his colleagues feel that the company's success was their success. His visionary, daring, and intuitive qualities helped him to keep focused on the goal, avoid short-term gratification and to aim for achievement. His open-mindedness helped the company and himself to develop and retain people with a variety of skills and attributes. This ensured new ideas and fresh approaches to problem solving. He surrounded himself with the best talent he could find and distributed leadership to allow his talented staff to grow and develop professionally. Both this CEO and Wayne, my principal at Lord Byron, "managed the dream."[6]

Real 'artists' create 'Big Hairy Audacious Goals' (BHAGS). "A BHAG is a huge and daunting goal – like a big mountain to climb. It is clear, compelling, and people 'get it' right away. A BHAG serves as a unifying focal point of effort, galvanizing people and creating team spirit as people strive towards a finish line."[7] Such goals are possible, not fantastic; understandable, not empty bravado; energising, not enervating. They include John F. Kennedy's challenge to land a man on the moon by the end of the Sixties, Ronald Reagan's strident call to Mr Gorbachev, to "bring down this wall", and Nelson Mandela's call for truth and reconciliation after years of personal imprisonment and national apartheid in South Africa.

Artists are the dreamers for whom the dreams, the BHAGS, are often more real than reality. We would have long forgotten Martin Luther King's moving 'I have a dream' speech if he had said 'I have a proposition' or 'I have a strategic plan'. We can all remember those immortal words:

> I have a dream that someday this nation will rise up and live out the true meaning of its creed: "We hold these truths to be self-evident that all men are created equal." I have a dream that one day on the red hills of Georgia the sons of former slaves and the sons of former slave owners will be able to sit down together at the table of brotherhood ... I have a dream that my four children will one day live in a nation where they will not be judged by the colour of their skin but by the content of their character.

Through rich imagery and metaphor, not cold facts and figures, he painted a picture of a more equitable future and galvanised both Black and White Americans in the cause of equal rights for all.

Similarly, recall the words of Winston Churchill in the darkest days of 1940 when few people, including the American ambassador to Britain Joseph Kennedy, gave Britain much of a chance to survive the Nazi onslaught. Shortly after the British retreat from Dunkirk, Churchill's radio address rallied his beleaguered nation with these powerful and emotive words:

> We shall not flag or fail. We shall go on to the end. We shall fight in France, we shall fight on the seas and the oceans, we shall fight with growing confidence and growing strength in the air, we shall defend our island, whatever the cost may be. We shall fight on the beaches, we shall fight on the landing grounds, we shall fight in the fields and in the streets, we shall fight in the hills; we shall never surrender.[8]

Churchill, the 'artist', held out a vision of a nation, united in its determination to resist the "odious apparatus of Nazi rule" and to persevere against the odds until such time as other nations, particularly the USA, came to its aid. He did not dwell on the terrible losses they had suffered, or the incredible odds that they faced, but offered a vision of hope and optimism. Just as King marched with his compatriots and suffered abuse and internment, Churchill also 'walked the talk'. After a German blitz, he would stroll through the shattered streets of London, encouraging, consoling and listening to the hopes and fears of his countrymen. In this, the 'darkest hour' for any nation, he successfully communicated his vision of ultimate victory and stirred his people to continue the fight. Churchill inspired because he made his followers believe that they collectively could overcome adversity. Hitler had a vision, but it was one of conquest that was so wrapped up in his own charismatic persona that the people of Germany believed that only through his leadership could they succeed, and without him they were lost. The historian Andrew Roberts[9] suggests that leaders, like Churchill, who develop a shared vision and create a collective attitude among their followers usually succeed, whereas the accomplishments of charismatic leaders like Hitler, who embody the vision in their person, tend to be short lived. True visionaries believe not only in goals that benefit themselves but also others.

Shared vision

While 'vision' is the accepted term, it is somewhat limiting because it suggests only a leader's visual or mental image of what he or she intends to achieve. In his interviews with progressive corporate leaders, Mihaly Csikszentmihalyi discovered that his leaders were driven by something "more visceral than a mental image. It involves feelings, and a sense of physical rootedness in a field of forces that includes the self but it is much larger." It is "a personal destiny, a calling."[10] Perhaps a better way of thinking about vision is to expand it to include voice, because it involves dialogue and must be shared before it can be a call to joint action. While school leadership is a long way from the leadership of nations and national and inter-national movements, the basic principles of leadership still apply. My former principal Wayne had a vision for Lord Byron that his col-leagues bought into. His vision became a shared vision that involved the voice of his colleagues. As one history teacher recalled, "the early years were inspiring. There was a lot of altruism. People came to work because they thought they were doing something for humanity – more than a job, it was a mission." One of his associates declared, "I became a teacher at Byron. I wrote more, I created from the ground up." One of my former female colleagues captured his 'artistry' this way:

> In retrospect, when I look back probably one of the things that made him a good leader was that he could talk about what you had done and say – he would remember and come back a couple of weeks later and say "how did such and such work out?" and I would say, it was either "great" or it "bombed". If it bombed, he would say "did all of it bomb or did only part of it bomb? Do you have to change it all?" It became a questioning routine so that it got you thinking again as to the evaluation of it and then you would start over again and make the changes you needed.

What I personally appreciated about his leadership was his willingness to take more than his share of the blame when things went wrong, and less than his share of the credit when things went right.[11] In many ways, Wayne would fit what the business writer Jim Collins[12] has described as a 'level five' leader. To Collins, a surprising finding of his extensive research on business organisations that were good but became great based on share returns over a sustained period of time was that the leaders of these companies embodied "a paradoxical mix of personal humility and professional will. They are ambitious, to be sure, but ambitious first and foremost for the company, not themselves."[13] These were not 'high-profile', charismatic, larger-than-life personalities, but rather quietly dedicated and persistent 'mortals' who achieved extraordinary results. Ironically, many of the so-called 'charismatic' leaders that they studied produced short-term gains, but failed to produce long-term greatness, often because they let their egos get in the way. In contemporary times, the take-over of Chrysler by Daimler-Benz and the sale of the *Daily Telegraph* in the UK are testimonials to the limits of the 'charismatic' leadership of such luminaries as Lee Iaccoca and Conrad Black!

Pitcher portrays, her third archetype, the 'craftsmen', as well-balanced individuals, trustworthy, reasonable, sensible and realistic. This was Garry. A mathematician and former engineer, he was long on common sense, persistence, and intellect. Garry prided himself on developing practical ways to 'make things work' – to make the impossible, possible. He knew that staff members must not only trust their leaders but also the systems that they put in place. Wayne wanted an individualised, semestered timetable to achieve his image of a school that responded to the needs, interests and abilities of each student.[14] This he believed would create greater flexibility for students to accelerate by taking extra courses in a semester or to pick up courses in which they had had difficulty. The problem was that no one had ever done this before, and this was at a time when computer technology was in its early stages. With the help of a former student, Garry worked out a way to do what many experts at the time considered impossible.

Wayne also had the idea that each student should receive an individualised report card from each of his or her teachers. In any given semester this meant getting over 80 teachers to manage 4,800 separate pieces of paper. Garry anticipated that this was potentially boring, tedious and confusing work for the teachers, so he invented the 'barn dance'. One cold late January morning, a grumpy group of teachers arrived at the school to distribute their report cards. Instead of drudgery, they were met with welcoming posters, hot coffee, juices, fruit and donuts. Upbeat music played in the background and Wayne and Garry, both wearing straw hats, welcomed the teachers with good humour and encouragement. Each semester for the next four years Garry refined the 'barn dance' so that a process that could have resulted in disgruntled teachers became an event that they eagerly anticipated. Years later, long after computer reporting replaced the need for the 'barn dance', teachers nostalgically related how much they missed the camaraderie and fun of the 'barn dance'.

Craftsmen

Craftsmen, like Garry, know what works and what doesn't. They help the 'artist' to bring to life a picture of an imagined but realistic future for the organisation. Craftsmen (and women)[15] understand that people make mistakes, but they can learn from them, and that it is folly to try to drive out error, because in doing so, you drive out innovation. Pitcher suggests that companies, and I would add schools and school districts, fail if they oust the unique vision of an 'artist' who the 'technocrats' consider to be 'unrealistic', 'impractical', 'airy-fairy' or worse, just plain 'loony'. Similarly, when 'experience' is linked with terms like 'outmoded' or 'old-fashioned' or 'out of date' as happened in Ontario in the late 1990s, 'technocrats' also drive out craftsmen who inspire the loyalty and dedication of others, and really understand the business of the organisation. What Garry shared with Wayne was an absolute commitment to ensuring Lord Byron's success. Some years after our time together, I occupied the office next door to Garry. I watched him turn the district's mediocre special education program into one of the best in Ontario. He accomplished this challenging task by remaining personally modest and 'low-key', but persistently, persuasively, and passionately advocating for students with special needs.

If as Pitcher argues, technocrats are brilliant at producing Sophisticated Measurable Annual Rigid Targets (SMARTS) then a craftsman like Garry produces challenging goals that wed the big picture thinking of the artist with a need for the short-term measurable results of the technocrat. Craftsmen develop and create an harmonious context, that motivates colleagues to pursue achievable, necessary, global, engaging, and sustainable goals for the organisation (CHANGES). Pitcher points out that running a modern company, and I would include a modern school or school district, requires "all kinds of perspectives ... even the cerebral, analytical and uncompromising. The Artists and Craftsmen can live with those different perspectives, but the Technocrat cannot."[16] Jim Collins[17] argues that his "good to great leaders" first made sure they had the right people in the right places in their leadership teams and then decided on directions and strategies, although this is much easier done in business than in education or the public service in general.

When Wayne hired his department chairs he intuitively built a team of different talents and abilities and gave them the authority and the time to do the job. As he stated:

> There is no doubt in my mind it was the chair. Leadership was one of the elements considered when the chairs[18] were chosen, and I believe it was an expectation that they understood, it was to be their leadership and their school, and in their areas they had control of programming and instruction[19] ... One of the significant factors was that chairmen had time to provide leadership to the people with whom they worked ... it demonstrated to me if you have an expectation for leadership you have to provide time to do the job.

While the working styles of the 'artist' and craftsman' may differ, not only can they coexist, they complement each other because they share a commitment to achieve sustainable, long-term, ambitious goals for their organisation. Wayne and Garry were on the right track in their pursuit of a humane school that responded to the needs of all students. They operated, however, within the paradigm of the time, Traditional Public Administration, in which inputs and processes were more important than results and district policies often circumscribed a school's autonomy. In the first decade of the twenty first century, they would now have to address the pressure for definable, measurable results. Looking back, I'm sure they would have welcomed the challenge because they had created a 'learning community' long before scholars popularised the concept.[20] To address the challenges of contemporary education, however, its leaders must be passionately, creatively, obsessively, and steadfastly committed to enhancing 'deep' learning for students – learning for understanding, learning for life, learning for a knowledge society.

High reliability organisations

While Byron was a student-centred school, schools of the twenty first century must become *student learning-centred* schools in which every structure, activity, policy or practice must contribute to students' learning or be abandoned or changed. When it comes to student learning there are no compromises; schools need to become High Reliability Organisations (HRO).[21] In a knowledge society, school dropouts will spend their lives in low paying jobs and experience exclusion from society's rewards. Like the failures of air traffic controllers, medical doctors, and nurses, educational failures can be disastrous for students and for society as a whole, and therefore educators must collectively bend every effort to become High Reliability Organisations for all students. 'No Child Left Behind', in the USA, is a wonderful and visionary goal and captures the essence of HRO, but the strategy attached to it is fatally flawed and in some ways counter productive.[22] Schools that are punished for their students' lack of achievement without consideration of context have the potential to negatively affect teacher commitment[23] which can result in the loss of quality teachers who become frustrated by conditions over which they have no control, moving to more affluent areas where the NCLB policies reward achievement. As a result, the school and the children they leave behind, usually in inner city neighbourhoods, become further depressed. Corcoran[24] explains that optimistic and constructive attitudes are more likely when teachers feel good about their work environment. "Policy makers need to listen very carefully to what teachers are saying about their working conditions".

I suggest as an alternative, an even bigger 'Hairy Audacious Goal' – 'No Child's Potential left Undeveloped'. How then as 'mere mortals' can leaders wed this big-picture 'audacious' goal to the demands of external testing, inspections, and review? I would suggest that the key for all leaders is to *commit* to successful learning for all students – not just the opportunity to learn, or to achieve great test scores, but a 'deep' and lasting learning for *all* students. This commitment is the keystone to effective school and district leadership and permeates everything that leaders do. How then does this commitment become 'habit-forming'?

Leaders of learning

First of all, we know that school principals and other school leaders respond to educational change in one of three predominant ways.[25]

1 Some wait until they have received specific orders and then respond. By using this coping style, they keep their backsides covered and when things go wrong they can blame the external sources of the change. This response has little to do with leadership; it has a great deal more to do with being a compliant messenger.

2 Others adopt a diffusion style – the 'Christmas tree'[26] approach. They want to hang whatever new bright and shiny innovative bauble (or change) that comes along on their tree (the school) so that outsiders will admire the school's progressivism, and these leaders can advance their careers. The trick for such leaders is to move on before the tree, or to be less metaphorical, the staff falls over from overload resulting in teacher resistance and cynicism towards future educational change.

3 The third pattern, goal-focused leadership, builds a community consensus around a few high-leverage, challenging goals and buffers the school and its teachers from outside pressures.[27] In student-learning centred schools, these goals concentrate on important aspects of student and/or teacher learning.

The third option, which is the only one consistent with a commitment to learning, requires leaders to understand and act on what is important in their schools or districts and to have the courage to resist the inevitable pressures to adopt outside initiatives. Leaders of learning develop the ability to 'say no slowly'. Let me explain by using an example. Let us first assume you have taken the time to build a consensus from the school's key stakeholders. Successful leaders take risks but not stupid risks; they do the politics first. You are now in a position to respond to an outside initiative. Seek answers to such questions as – how does this innovation or change fit our existing agreed upon goals? Does this innovation have funding for three years? Does this innovation have long-term political support? Is our school ready to proceed on a new venture? If the answers to these questions are 'no', then that is the time to say, "thank you very much for the offer, I'm sure it (your innovation) will be a great success, but we have other priorities." While this may sound like fantasy, one of the principals in our study delayed the implementation of a government-mandated program for two years until he and his colleagues had put other more urgent priorities in place. It took courage and the backing of a strongly supportive staff and community, but it is possible to say 'no' slowly.

Secondly, leaders of learning focus on the standards that are important. Standards will not go away, nor should they. Standards answer the question for students, "what do I have to know and be able to do to succeed?", and for teachers they answer the question of "what should I teach and expect of my students?" The problem for students and teachers, however, is the 'over-stuffed curriculum'. Michael White describes the American experience with standards this way:

> When standards were introduced, we never stopped teaching what we had already been teaching. We tried to add standards to the school day and our workload. Big mistake! Most research shows that American teachers are already trying to cover too much material. Fourth grade teachers in Japan are content to cover 17 math topics. And they have 250 days of school in which to do it. In Singapore it's against the law to adopt a text-book with more than 100 pages. Compare that to America where the educational mantra is still "finish the book." And the bigger the book the better. Fourth grade teachers here scurry to cover on average 78 topics in a 180-day school year. That comes out to a little more than two days per topic.[28]

His associate Douglas Reeves suggests that schools and school leaders should help teachers to identify 'power standards':

> Power Standards are prioritised standards that are derived from a systematic and balanced approach to distinguishing the standards that are absolutely essential for student success from those that are "nice to know." Power Standards are a subset of the complete list of standards for each grade and for each subject. They represent the "safety net" of standards that each teacher needs to make sure that every student learns prior to leaving the

current grade. Students who acquire this "safety net" of knowledge and skills will thus exit one grade better prepared for the next grade.[29]

Leaders of learning help teachers to determine the standards that all students 'must know' – 'the power standards'. But they don't stop there. They work with their teacher colleagues to help each child achieve his or her potential by identifying a second category of standards beyond the basics that I would call 'necessary to know', and finally the more esoteric advanced 'learnings' that Reeves describes as 'nice to know'. Good standards tell students what is required for them to achieve at each level by delineating rubrics of performance criteria that are in turn connected to assessment strategies. Student-learning centred schools not only prepare their students to achieve by assessments *of* their learning, but also to use assessment *for* learning and *as* learning. There is an increasingly powerful body of evidence that suggests, "that teaching for understanding of the concepts and processes lies at the heart of the subject and trusts that deeper understanding will inevitably produce better test performances."[30] In student-learning centred schools leaders and teachers not only ensure that students achieve the mandated standards required for credentialing their achievements, they use alternative assessment strategies to help students become the kind of self-directed learners that the knowledge economy demands.[31]

The contemporary emphasis on summative modes of assessment tends to discount conceptual or 'deep' learning, and focuses more on factual material, or materials that test-producers can package conveniently and inexpensively. Traditional assessments *of* learning often assess only limited samples of the results or destinations of learning rather than the students' entire intellectual journey where 'deep learning' takes place. Examination of a student's learning odyssey, 'assessment *for* learning', provides a more authentic, challenging and interactive approach to student assessment and learning because it focuses as much on the trip as the target. It maintains a reciprocal relationship between student and teacher in which the teacher's role becomes that of a guide rather than that of a judge and executioner. Students assess and revise their work throughout a unit of study by incorporating worksheets and checklists among other strategies to ensure their work is meeting curricular standards. Teachers are still central players in assessment *for* learning, but they use the context of the assessment and the curriculum standards to identify particular learning needs. Within this framework of such formative assessment, teachers in student-learning centred schools provide students with the feedback and guidance to review, revise, or rewrite their work. In this way students have an opportunity to discuss concepts with their teachers, to delve more deeply into underlying meanings, to discuss and explore interesting and creative new avenues of learning without the fear of failure. The teacher can point the student towards more fruitful areas of study, frame new questions, investigate alternative theories, and work co-operatively to master the concepts and complete the assignment to meet and even surpass the expected standards. Assessment of this nature includes such strategies as portfolios, journals and workbooks that students complete co-operatively with their teachers and fellow students.[32]

Assessment *as* learning holds even more promise for students' learning because it places more of the responsibility of learning squarely on the shoulders of students themselves. This approach to assessment challenges students to monitor their own work and to ask questions and clarify ideas for themselves. In their own lives, there will not always be someone there to tell students what to do, or what to think, and assessment as learning develops prior knowledge and uses it as a basis for learning. "Students are active, engaged and critical assessors, they can make sense of information, relate it to prior knowledge and master the skills involved."[33] The role of the teacher is to act as a co-strategist who offers suggestions on how students can reach conclusions for themselves. By assuming responsibility for their own achievement, students learn to organise, create, evaluate, and 'think outside the box'. Assessment *as* learning is an 'audacious' idea that is consistent with the demands of a knowledge society and arguably helps students to not only achieve basics standards but to surpass them. The challenge for leaders of student-learning centred schools, however, is to promote deep, lasting and engaging learning experiences for students within a policy regimen in most jurisdictions that is more interested in predictability, control and compliance.

While 'designer' leadership and current approaches to educational change described in Chapter 1 may arguably deliver a pre-packaged, top-down reform agenda, they have limited currency when it comes to preparing students for a knowledge society in which "human creativity is the ultimate economic resource."[34] Traditional white-collar and blue-collar jobs are either disappearing or migrating to developing countries. Economic prosperity now depends on our society's ability to encourage and develop people who are creative, imaginative, innovative and entrepreneurial – 'artists' and 'craftsmen'.

Leaders of student-learning centred schools may have little influence over government-mandated standards and accountability measures, but most government reform packages provide schools and teachers with considerable discretion as to how they assist students to achieve the standards. My observation of curriculum standards in many jurisdictions is that they are not as restrictive as the professionals believe. How teachers shape the curriculum, construct their lessons, design follow-up assignments and homework, organise their classrooms, and challenge their students intellectually provides plenty of scope for them to be creative and in turn encourage their students to be creative and innovative and to address real-life issues. Leaders of student-learning centred schools assist their teachers to engage their students both intellectually and emotionally, assess for learning and assess as learning, and develop programs that promote creativity and ingenuity. They also ensure that courses and curriculum units in the arts, physical and vocational education that encourage student resourcefulness and inventiveness receive appropriate emphasis in students' overall programs.

Conclusion

The compelling argument for educational change presented by policy makers in virtually every school jurisdiction that I have visited over the past ten years (state, province, city) links educational improvement with economic competitiveness in the international globalised marketplace. While this is a powerful argument for change, it is not the only rationale for educational change. Schools have a larger role than just preparing students to make a living and provide human capital to national, provincial or state economies; they also groom students for life. We had this viewpoint confirmed as part of our Change Frames project.[35] One February morning in

1998, the principal of Talisman Park Secondary School invited 70 'stakeholders' to meet in the school's library to consider the school's purposes for the ensuing five years. This group included teachers, students, parents, school-board members, business people from the community, leaders of ethnic communities, clerics, local and provincial politicians, and other interested participants. Through an interactive process, the assembled delegates arrived at three overriding goals for the school. In addition to 'preparation for working life' and 'preparation for life long learning', they also included 'preparation for positive social interaction'. Woven throughout these three broad goals, the assembled group, and particularly the parents, stressed the need for students to develop 'a positive outlook', 'emotional intelligence', 'self-management', 'confidence', 'self-esteem', and 'tolerance' among many other personal competencies.

What Wayne and Garry, 'artists' and 'craftsmen'[36], and the 'good to great leaders'[37] all share is a passionate commitment to achieving the goals of the organisation. What makes education so exciting and crucial, is that we as educators touch the face of the future, so we must commit ourselves to achieving learning goals such as those described by the Talisman Park community that are humane, life affirming, 'audacious', comprehensive and bold. The international corporation, The Body Shop, in one of its many publications, captured the need for such learning goals when it declared:

Let's help our children to develop the habit of freedom. To encourage them to celebrate who and what they are.

Let's stop teaching children to fear change and protect the status quo. Let's teach them to enquire and debate. To ask questions until they hear answers. And the way to do it is to change the way of our traditional schooling.

Our educational system does its best to ignore and suppress the creative spirit of children. It teaches them to listen unquestioningly to authority. It insists that education is just knowledge contained in subjects and the purpose of education is to get a job. What's left out is sensitivity to others, non-violent behavior, respect, intuition, imagination, and a sense of awe and wonderment.[38]

Leaders of learning-centred schools not only understand the challenges of their contexts, and commit totally to ensuring such learning for all their students, they possess a philosophy, a mind set, 'a story', a 'stance', a value system which guides all of their leadership activities. Chapter 3 proposes a value position to which 'mere mortals' can subscribe and use to guide their leadership activities.

Notes

1   Lord Byron, *School Priorities*, 1974–75, p. 1.
2   Leadbetter, C. (2004). *Learning about Personalisation: How can we put the learner at the heart of the education system?* Nottingham: Department for Education and Skills.
    Tarleton, R. (2004). 'Bespoke learning', *Innovations*. Personalised Learning: Special Ldr., supplement, pp: 3–5.
3   Lord Byron Evaluation Committee (1975). *Report of Lord Byron Evaluation Committee*. p. 20.
4   Ibid. p. 20.
5   Pitcher (1997) op. cit.
6   Bennis, W. (2000). *Managing the Dream: Reflections on leadership and change*. Cambridge, MA: Perseus Publishing.
7   Collins, J. (2001). *Good to Great: Why some companies make the leap and others don't*. New York: Harper Business, p. 202.
8   Radio broadcast on 4 June 1940.
9   Roberts, A. (2003). *Hitler and Churchill: Secrets of leadership*. London: Weidenfeld & Nicolson.
10 Csikszentmihalyi, M. (2004). *Good Business: Leadership flow and the making of meaning*. New York: Penguin Books, p. 197.
11 Williams, P. (2002). *Paradox of Power: A transforming view of leadership*. New York: Warner/Faith.
12 Collins, J. (2001) op. cit., p. 202.
13 Collins, J. (2001) op. cit., p. 30.
14 Lord Byron was the first semestered school in Ontario. A student's program required eight courses in a year. Teachers usually taught six 40-minute periods in a day. In Lord Byron's semester system, each student was required to be in class for four 60-minute periods in a day for half of the school year, and to follow the same format in the second semester. Teachers taught four, 60-minute periods in a day. Over half of the schools in Ontario are still semestered.
15 I have stayed with Pitcher's (1997, op.cit) term 'craftsmen' to avoid awkward and excessive verbiage, but this term certainly includes the many outstanding women leaders I have worked with over the years.

16 Pitcher (1997) op. cit., p. 69.

17 Collins, J. op cit., p. 41.

18 Byron's departments were organised into cross-disciplinary units such as Social Sciences, the Arts, Mathematics, Science and Technology, with a department chair in charge as opposed to a department head. The number of formal leaders was therefore reduced from as many as 22 in some schools to ten. The major role of the department chair was to support the classroom teachers. They also formed the principal's cabinet to work out school policies and procedures and make sure that teachers were informed and had input on school issues.

19 This term for teaching is more prevalent in Canada and the USA.

20 For a more detailed description of Lord Byron as a learning community see Fink, D. (2000) *Good Schools/Real Schools: Why school reforms don't last*. New York: Teachers' College Press.

21 Stringfield, S. (1995). 'Attempts to enhance students' learning: A search for valid programs and highly reliable implementation techniques', *School Effectiveness and School Improvement*, 6 (1): pp: 67–96.

22 Kohn, A. (2004). 'Test today, privatise tomorrow: Using accountability to "reform" public schools to death', *Phi Delta Kappa* 85 (8): pp: 569–77; Harvery, J. (2003) 'The Matrix Reloaded', *Educational Leadership*, 61 (3): pp: 18–21; Linn, R. (2003) 'Accountability, responsibility and reasonable expectations', *Educational Researcher*, 32 (7): pp: 3–13.

23 See Mintrop, H. (2003). 'The limits of sanctions in low performing schools: A study of low performing schools of Maryland and Kentucky Schools on probation', *Education Policy Analysis Archive*, 11(3): at www.epaa.asu.edu/epaa/v11n3.html

24 Corcoran, T.B. (1990). 'Schoolwork: Perspectives on workplace reform in public schools', in M.W. McLaughlin, J.E. Talbert and N. Bascia (eds), *The Contexts of Teaching in Secondary Schools: Teachers' realities*. New York: Teachers' College Press, pp. 142–66.

25 Tye, B. (2000). *Hard Truths: Uncovering the deep structures of schooling*. New York: Teachers' College Press.

26 Bryk, A.S. et al. (1993*). A View from the Elementary Schools: The state of reform in Chicago*. Chicago, IL: Consortium on School Research.

27 Tye, B. and Tye, K. (1992). *Global Education: A study of school change*. Albany, NY: State University of New York Press.

28 White, M. (2004). 'Why we hate standards', Center for Performance Assessment: monthly newsletter, July, at www.MakingStandardsWork.com

29 Reeves, D. (2004). at www.makingstandardswork.com/professional_development/power_standards.htm

30 See Nuthall, G. and Alton-Lee, A. (1995). 'Assessing Classroom Learning: How students use their knowledge and experience to

answer classroom achievement test questions in science and social studies', in *American Educational Research Journal*, 32 (1): pp: 185–223; Boaler, J. (1997) *Experiencing School Mathematics: Teaching styles, sex and setting*. Buckingham, UK: Open University Press; Newman, R.S., Bryk, A.S. and Nagaoka, J.K. (2001) *Authentic Intellectual Work and Standardized Tests: Conflicts and coexistence*. Chicago, IL: Consortium on Chicago School Research; Black, P. and Williams, D. (2004) 'The formative purpose: Assessment must first promote learning', in M.Wilson (ed.), *Towards Coherence Between Classroom Assessment and Accountability: 103rd Yearbook of the National Society for the Study of Education*. Chicago, IL: Chicago University Press; Reeves, D. (2004) *Accountability for Learning: How teachers and schools can take charge*. Alexandria, VA: Association for Supervision and Curriculum Development.

31 Earl, L. (2004). *Assessment as Learning: Using classroom assessment to maximize student learning*. Thousand Oaks, CA: Corwin.

32 Ibid.

33 Ibid. p. 25.

34 Florida, R. (2002). *The Rise of the Creative Class: How it's transforming work, leisure, community, and everyday life*. New York: Basic Books, p. xv.

35 Hargreaves, A., Shaw, P., Fink, D., Retallick, J., Giles, C., Moore, S., Schmidt, M. and James-Wilson, S. (2000). *Change Frames: Supporting secondary teachers in interpreting and integrating secondary school reform*. Toronto, ON: Ontario Institute for Studies in Education/University of Toronto.

36 Pitcher (1997) op. cit.

37 Collins (2001) op. cit.

38 Publication of the Body Shop.

3   *Values*

I remember Harold as though it was yesterday. I first saw him when my wife, daughter and I checked into a dormitory at the University of Western Carolina, which is located in Cullowhee, North Carolina, a beautiful little university town nestled in the glorious Smokey Mountains. Both Harold and I were among 60 educators from Canada and the USA that the then Dean of Education had invited to a summer institute on something called Invitational Education. I have to admit now, many years later, that I was tired after a long year and had come there more for an inexpensive holiday than intellectual enlightenment or cultural stimulation. Little did I know at the time how much Harold and the two weeks in Cullowhee would influence my thinking and career.

Harold was a tall man of indeterminate age who had obviously suffered from an horrendous accident. He had no fingers on either hand, and his face and arms were terribly mottled and disfigured from severe burns. On the first evening after registration, the university had arranged a 'square dance' party to welcome participants to Cullowhee. When we arrived we noticed Harold sitting by himself in a corner. My eleven year old daughter announced to us that she was going to ask him to dance. I asked her if she was not put off by his appearance whereupon she gave me one of those 'don't be stupid' looks that children can give their parents, and went over and introduced herself to Harold. She invited him to dance, and he accepted. She danced at least four times with Harold and sat and chatted with him for a considerable length of time. On the way back to the residence, I told her that I was proud of the way she had invited him to join the festivities and asked her why she had made that decision. She replied, "I liked his eyes and I liked his voice."

A few days later, Harold told his story to the group. While a member of the American National Guard, a methane gas explosion had killed 20 of Harold's fellow soldiers and seriously injured many more. He had suffered the most serious injuries of those who had survived. Since that awful day, he had gone through over 200 surgical procedures. In one of the more remarkable operations, doctors surgically reconstructed his lips. He told us that in those early days after the accident, as he lay in excruciating pain in his hospital bed, deaf and blind, he knew he could choose life or death. He chose life because of the love and empathy he felt from his family and friends who virtually willed him to live. Now that his health had improved, he had decided that he would return to school to earn a postgraduate degree in counselling so that he could counsel other burn victims. His teacher, William Purkey, had suggested that this course on Invitational Education might help his re-entry into society because of the kind of people it attracted.

For me the week in Cullowhee was a significant turning point in my own psychological growth. I learned from Harold, my daughter Tracy, and the other participants, about the meaning and power of 'invitations'. From Harold, I learned that in extreme situations invitations can mean the difference between life and death and can provide the incentive to continue on in the face of overwhelming difficulties. From Tracy, I understood at a much deeper level the meaning of an invitation. By having the courage to ask Harold to dance and then proceeding to spend time with him at the dance and during the following weeks, she extended to Harold, both verbally and non-verbally, invitations that communicated to him that he was a valuable person. Others, as Purkey had anticipated, rallied around Harold and made him feel welcomed, and a part of the group. For all of us in attendance in Cullowhee, the formal definition of an invitation that we learned in the seminars – an invitation is a summary description of messages, formal and informal, verbal and non-verbal, continuously transmitted to others to inform them that they are able, valuable and responsible[1] – became more than just carefully crafted words; its meaning became a lived experience.

Invitations

Over the course of the next two weeks, as the instructors explained the philosophical and psychological roots of invitational education

I began to make connections and see relationships and issues that I had struggled with over a number of years. By looking at everything that goes on in a school as 'messages' that communicate 'meanings', I began to look at the interpersonal relationships, the culture, the policies, practices, programs, micro-politics and structures in the schools that I worked with in a new light. What messages did they send? Did they invite people by communicating that you are able, valuable and responsible or did they intentionally or unintentionally communicate negative messages or 'disinvitations'?

For example, in one of the secondary schools in which I taught the principal assigned three of my colleagues and myself to supervise the cafeteria to ensure cleanliness and order. Ashamed to say, we called it 'pig patrol' and sure enough in spite of our best efforts the cafeteria usually ended up looking like pigs had inhabited it. At Lord Byron and later as principal of my own school we instituted a policy of informal supervision. In both situations the principal and a number of the teachers would eat lunch in the main cafeteria with the students, even though there was a separate teachers' cafeteria available. On occasion, as principal, I would sit with different groups of students and initiate discussions on how things were going in the school. The purposes in these two scenarios were similar – to maintain tidiness and order – but the messages communicated to the students were quite different. In the 'pig patrol' circumstance, we expected the students to make a mess and be disorderly and thus, unintentionally, communicated that message with the result that they more than lived up to our expectation. In the second scenario, the message communicated was that 'we think as young adults you are responsible', and in practice the cafeteria was generally tidy and orderly. Informal cafeteria supervision gave me, as principal of the school, an excellent way to get to know the students in a relaxed setting and also to seek out problems before they became problems to solve.

One of the principals who reported to me, Paul, led a large secondary school of 1,600 students. When I would visit him as his superintendent (inspector), he would insist that I join him to walk the halls at period breaks. I cannot prove it but he seemed to know every student's name. He had a large rotating file sitting prominently on his desk in which he had stored every student's picture, name and key details such as birth date. When it was a student's birthday he would personally go to the student's classroom and present a small gift. In a large school this was no mean feat. He modelled the invitational approach for teachers rather than preaching and exhorting. Conversely, the principal of a small elementary school that I knew well called every boy, 'buddy' and every girl 'sweetheart'. You could almost see the girls cringe when this 50-something principal called them 'sweetheart'. He was just too lazy and indifferent to bother to learn names. While he was not intentionally 'disinviting', the students clearly understood his message of disinterest and they in turn treated him with a total lack of respect. Invitational education, therefore, "provides a framework for thinking about who we are and what we hope to accomplish in education" by examining the 'meanings' behind our 'messages' and creating "a total school environment that intentionally summons success for everyone associated with the school."[2]

Robert Shapiro, the former chairman and Chief Executive Officer of the Monsanto corporation applied the idea of invitations to leadership this way:

> I don't really believe in traditional power in large organizations, because I don't think it works very well ... You are in a position to start conversations. You are in a position to influence what people will talk about, and think about. And from that point on, what effect it has is a direct function of the quality of the conversations you initiated. It either resonates with people, appeals to something that matters to them, or it doesn't. It either feels authentic to them and feels like something they genuinely want to engage in, or it doesn't. And there is no way of compelling it. It's an invitation.[3]

Invitational leadership

Over eight years ago, my colleague Louise Stoll and I tried to capture the idea of invitations in our first attempt to define 'invitational leadership' in educational terms. We stated that, "Leadership is about communicating invitational messages to individuals and groups with whom the leader interacts in order to build and act on a shared and evolving vision of enhanced educational experiences for pupils."[4] We would now modify our definition only slightly to capture a school's core purpose as described in Chapter 2. "Leadership is about communicating invitational messages to individuals and groups with whom the leader interacts in order to build and act on a shared and evolving vision of a *learning-centred* school." This definition is predicated on a set of interrelated and interconnected values – trust, respect, optimism and intentionality – that provide a foundation or touchstone for leaders in good times and in bad.

Trust

The starting point for any relationship is *trust*. Think of any relationship that you have entered into and the fundamental question that you have probably consciously or unconsciously asked yourself is "what kind of person are you?" You ask it of your local politicians, your television repairman, your doctor, your plumber and so on. As a five year old child meeting your first teacher, or as a first year teacher meeting your principal, or as a parent meeting your child's teacher for the first time, you have wondered "Can I trust you?"

In fact the very foundation of a civil society is trust. Can we trust our political leaders, our business community, our educators, or the press? The erosion of trust can have serious consequences. The Enron and MCI scandals in the USA have seriously undermined trust in the economic system and particularly in large multinational corporations. In fact, even before the Enron fiasco only 47 per cent of the employees surveyed in American companies believed their corporate leaders were people of integrity. Moreover, 58 per cent of these employees thought that top executives were out for themselves, and only 33 per cent thought that top executives were interested in advancing the interests of their organisations.[5] Bill Clinton's lies about his sexual activities, and the misinformation that has resulted in the USA and the UK making the decisions to invade Iraq have seriously shaken society's trust in the politicians and the intelligence communities in both countries. The political partisanship of some television news channels and print media has produced scepticism and cynicism especially among younger people. The tragic cases of the abuse of trusting children by clerics have eroded trust in the most sacred of our institutions. As Kouzes and Posner report, in the USA "the cynics are winning. The regard for leaders from all organized groups – politics, government, business, labor, and the church – is so low that they are no longer paid much heed. And lack of confidence has led people to be less willing to participate in the struggle to improve."[6]

It is therefore ironic that governments intent on educational improvement throughout the western world, with the assistance of a compliant press, have systemically attempted to undermine trust bonds between schools and their communities. For example, the Chief Inspector of Schools for England and Wales under both John Major and Tony Blair habitually named and blamed teachers for every real and imagined ill in the system. If his efforts were intended to motivate, his strategy backfired. "You can't make people winners by calling them losers."[7] When relationships go wrong the way to start to rebuild is with trust, which is not always easy. Rebuilding that trust bond with teachers and parents has proven to be a very difficult task for the UK government.

"Honesty is absolutely essential to leadership. If people are going to follow someone willingly, whether it is into battle or into the boardroom, they want to assure themselves that the person is worthy of trust."[8] In their study of the characteristics of America's most admired leaders, Kouzes and Posner reported that 83 per cent of their respondents rated honesty as the most important quality for business leaders.[9] There is ample evidence[10] that social trust is a key ingredient for school improvement. The only way I know to engender trust is to be absolutely trustworthy. Personal integrity was a quality I valued in others and sought to model in my own practice. Predictability is a key element of trust, and 'trustworthy' leaders try to behave consistently and authentically. One of my abilities (or disabilities) is to become totally absorbed by my own thoughts. It is a wonderful habit when writing a book, but others (including wives and children) can find it very annoying. I can recall instances where teachers have come to me and asked if for some reason they had upset me because I had walked right past them without extending my usual greeting. I would then have to apologise profusely and explain that I was so consumed by certain issues that I really did not see them. These episodes taught me the fragility of trust and the need for consistency in my own behaviour.

Warren Bennis explains that a significant role for leaders is the management of trust, and the keys to trusting relationships are "constancy and focus." He contends that "people would rather follow individuals they can count on, even when they disagree with their viewpoint, than people they agree with but shift their positions frequently."[11] Not only do they want constancy and focus in their interpersonal relationships but they want to be able to trust the policies and practices initiated by the leader. "Teachers want supportive work conditions for their practice, which depends on the capacity of the school principal to fairly, effectively and efficiently manage school operations."[12] Similarly, parents trust principals and teachers that are constant, competent and caring in their pursuit of student learning. Trusting relationships are also respectful relationships.

Respect

If you think back to that first encounter with a teacher, or the new principal, or your entry into any other important relationship you intuitively asked the question "how much do you understand me and genuinely care?" Students felt that my friend Paul who knew all their names genuinely cared about them. The students who the principal called 'buddy' and 'sweetheart' felt disrespected and behaved accordingly towards him. We all need to be acknowledged as the unique people we are, to be viewed as able, valuable and responsible human beings, not just cogs in a machine or numbers to be processed or human capital. We all need invitations. Unfortunately, our hurried society has little time to listen to us or even acknowledge our uniqueness and humanity. Pressures of inspections, high stakes tests, aggressive parents, misbehaving students and so on, can sometimes get in the way of showing respect to colleagues, students and other key stakeholders. Educators are not alone in feeling harried. In their study of what followers look for in their leaders in the business community, Kouzes and Posner[13] report that the quality that followers demand of their leaders that showed the most significant increase from the 1980s to the 1990s is supportiveness – people "require more understanding and help from their leaders." Perhaps the best way to show respect is to follow Steven Covey's[14] advice to seek first to understand and then to be understood. Mark Koenig[15] offers these suggestions to business people that I have adapted for school leaders:

- Stand behind the decisions your colleagues make.

- Sit down and talk things over with your colleagues.

- Let your colleagues feel free to ask you to reconsider a decision.

- Create opportunities for colleagues to air their opinions.

- Listen to your colleagues' personal problems that could affect their work.

- Compliment people on their work.

- Make it easy for colleagues to feel they're on top of what they're doing.

- Allow your colleagues to offer constructive criticism without fear of reprisal.

- Give your colleagues full credit for ideas they contribute at work so they will feel more part of the organisation.

- Make suggestions that will help colleagues improve their work.

While these suggestions are useful for competent colleagues, how does the notion of invitational leadership deal with incompetence? If we subscribe to the core purpose for schools as focusing on student learning, then leaders cannot tolerate incompetence or mediocre performance. I have dealt with a number of teachers in my career who for whatever reason were not suited to work with students, as well as principals and assistants who could not handle the challenges of leadership. All of the people I dealt with were very decent and hard working people with abilities, but ill suited for the jobs they had chosen. Most school jurisdictions have carefully prescribed, legally written procedures for demotion or dismissal that are time consuming and usually quite demeaning to the person whose performance is under review. I found that an informal, non-threatening invitational approach that showed respect for the individual reflected an understanding of his or her personal and professional circumstances, and providing help and support for a career change allowed the person to leave with dignity, and the school to find an appropriate replacement.

For example, Allan was the assistant principal in one of the schools that I supervised. At one point in his career he had aspired to become a principal but he could never get an appointment, and had settled into the assistant's role. His performance had deteriorated over the years. He did the managerial aspects of the job adequately, but was certainly not a 'leader of learning'. His principal had worked with him to improve his performance but the 'spark' just wasn't there. When I met with him I asked him "are you having any fun in your job?" He said he really didn't find it terribly rewarding. I asked him "when was the last time you really looked forward to coming to school?", and he replied that it was when he taught middle school mathematics. I said to him, "if I can find a middle school mathematics job for you and 'grandfather'[16] your salary so that you don't receive a salary cut would you accept it?" His face lit up and he replied, "gladly". I was able to find him a job in another school with a very supportive principal and Allan spent the last eight years of his career as a happy, and from all reports, very successful mathematics teacher.

The leadership challenge is first to determine if indeed the person is in fact poorly suited to the task, or just the wrong person in the wrong place at the wrong time. Then assuming performance is unacceptable and student learning is suffering, is the cost in terms of time and energy to improve this person's performance and the fallout for students as he or she works through the improvement process worth it? If not, then how can we find ways to allow the person to leave the job with dignity? Respect involves responding to colleagues' essential needs, even those who under-perform. Glasser says we have four basic needs: to care and feel cared for; to have some power over one's circumstance; to have hope for the future; and to have fun.[17] Respect involves caring and empowerment; optimism incorporates hope and fun.

Optimism

The former mayor of New York, Rudolph Giuliani,[18] during and immediately after the 9/11 catastrophe, states in his book *Leadership* that

It's up to the leader to instill confidence, to believe in his judgement and in people even when they no longer believe in themselves. Sometime the optimism of the leader is grounded in something only he knows – the situation isn't as dire as people think for reasons that will eventually become clear. But sometimes the leader has to be optimistic simply because if he isn't no one else will be. And you have to at least fight back no matter how daunting the odds.

Kouzes and Posner[19] report that 'forward-looking' leadership is what people look for in their leaders after 'honesty'. They want to know their leaders have vision, a sense of direction, and a destination. The teacher you worshipped, the principal you admired, the university professor you tried to emulate, responded either explicitly or implicitly to your need to get answers to such conscious or unconscious questions as, "Do you know where you are going?", "Is it a trip worth taking?", "Am I invited to go along?" They responded to your hopes at the time, and quieted your fears. They made the journey enjoyable if not outright fun.

When I worked for Wayne, he made the job fun. I've never worked so hard in my life, but I loved it. Every Friday we would adjourn to the local pub – all 80 of us, whether we took a drink or not, and it wasn't to make sure people didn't talk about us. After a few drinks, when he felt suitably loquacious, he would give a little speech in which he would tell us about the good things he had seen in the school. Over the course of a few weeks he would acknowledge virtually everyone on the staff. He always told us that our job was "to catch the kids doing something good" and to build on that. In his own practice, he managed by walking around the school and catching us doing something good, and then acknowledging what he saw and heard. His record for producing school and district leaders remains unparalleled in the district in which we worked. He was what Napoleon called "a dealer in hope". He encouraged our initiatives, helped us to learn from our failures, and never let us forget our commitment to the students.

At the same time he didn't engage in a Pollyanna-like false optimism. He dealt with activities and behaviours that were inconsistent with the school's avowed purposes in a respectful but thorough way. He did not let issues fester until they became full-blown problems. We could usually tell from his sober mood when the school was under attack and we would consequently rally around him. Infrequently he would show anger over unprofessional behaviour that sent a message to everyone. As Goleman and his colleagues[20] explain:

> Although emotions and moods may seem trivial ... they have real consequences for getting work done ... a sober mood can help immensely when considering a risky situation – too much optimism can lead to ignoring danger ... While mild anxiety can focus attention and energy, prolonged distress can sabotage a leader's relationships and can also hamper work performance ... A good laugh or upbeat mood on the other hand, more often enhances the neural abilities crucial for good work.

At a school level, Sergiovanni[21] asserts that placing "hope at the centre of our school community provides encouragement and promotes clear thinking and informed action, giving us the leverage we need to close the achievement gap and solve other intractable problems." However, he discriminates between hope that is grounded in realism and wishful thinking that takes no deliberate action to make wishes come true. The key to hopeful or optimistic leadership, therefore, is intentionally to develop a systematic approach to school improvement. It is 'intentionality', the fourth of the invitational values or principles, that gives trust, respect and optimism their purpose and direction.

Intentionality

Invitations are about intentions and they are about choices. In the anecdote that initiated this chapter I described how my daughter Tracy chose to invite Harold to dance and intentionally set out to communicate to him that he was a valuable person. Perhaps it was his eyes or voice, but she felt she could trust him; she demonstrated respect by the very act of approaching him, and she did so in a spirit of hope and optimism. Without her intentional action of inviting him to dance, however, her feelings of trust, respect and optimism would have only led to well-meaning but unrealised intentions and perhaps guilt at an opportunity missed. Invitations are not risk free.

Harold might have felt uncomfortable dancing with an 11 year old child and, as was his right, could have turned my daughter down, which probably would have been very hurtful for her. Perhaps he sensed her trusting attitude and fortunately for both he chose to accept. Once again, nice story, so what? It clearly illustrates the potential and payoffs of intentional invitations as well as the chances one takes and the risks one assumes when extending or accepting invitations.

Good intentions are not enough. They must be acted upon. Intentionality is the engine that engages invitational leaders and their colleagues in developing and sustaining actionable plans that promote student learning within a values-based framework. Without intentionality, stated values become rather hollow or worse. For example, Jeffrey Skillings, disgraced former head of Enron, described his job as "doing God's work." His successor, Ken Lay, who the US Justice Department indicted for various breaches of trust, stated that "one of the most satisfying things in life is to create a high moral and ethical environment in which every individual is allowed and encouraged to realize that God-given potential." These are wonderful sentiments but more than a bit hypocritical when actions do not support them.[22]

A theory of everything

From an educational leadership perspective, an invitational framework provides a 'theory of action' based on four unchanging core premises:

1 Education is a co-operative, collaborative activity where process is as important as product.

2 People are able, valuable, and responsible, and should be treated accordingly.

3 People possess untapped potential in all areas of human endeavour.

4 Human potential can best be realised by creating a total school culture specifically designed to invite development, and by

people who are intentionally inviting of themselves and others, personally and professionally.[23]

Collins and Porras in their study of highly successful business organisations concluded that:

> the essence of a visionary company (school, district) comes in the translation of its core ideology and its own unique drive for progress into the very fabric of the organization – into goals, strategies, tactics, policies, processes, cultural practices, management behaviors, building layouts, pay systems, accounting systems, job designs – into everything that the company does. A visionary company (school, district) creates a total environment that envelops employees (students, teachers, parents, support services etc.), bombarding them with a set of signals so consistent and mutually reinforcing that it's virtually impossible to misunderstand the company's ideology and ambitions.[24]

From this perspective, the invitational framework has the potential to be more than a theory of action, a 'theory of everything'. The first test of a 'theory of everything' for a school or district is – does it enhance the learning of all students? Does it conform to our fundamental purpose – student learning? The second test is – does it fit our core values? Does it communicate to our students, teachers, parents and other key stakeholders, that they are able, valuable and responsible? When we organise our schools to create separate tracks (streams, bands) are we promoting learning for *all* students? What messages are we communicating to the students and teachers in each of the tracks? When we decide to cut the budget for the arts and increase the science budget, what are we actually saying about the purposes of education and about those students who may thrive in the arts but struggle in science? This invitational 'theory of everything' obliges us as educators to reflect on the messages behind our actions, and more importantly to intentionally invite all students to learn in a climate of trust, respect, optimism, and intentionality.

Rooted in perceptual psychology and self-concept theory,[25] invitational leadership is a cohesive and holistic approach to leadership with four pillars to provide its structure:

- inviting oneself personally;

- inviting others personally;

- inviting oneself professionally;

- inviting others professionally.

Attending to our own personal and professional growth and building supportive and respectful relationships with others are prerequisites to developing professional learning communities that promote student learning.

Inviting oneself personally

I was sitting on the couch in our family room with one of my daughters one evening and she turned to me and said, "what are you doing here?" I replied that in case she hadn't noticed "I live here". Her response was "what happened? Couldn't you find a meeting to go to?" Her comment hit me between the eyes. My job was not only consuming my working day, but many evenings, and more than a few weekends. My daughter's remark forced me to rethink some of my choices. As I reflected, I realised that I was, in the words of Steven Covey, "deep in the thick of thin things."[26] I had unintentionally failed to take enough time to attend to my loved ones or to look after me. I found myself in that uncomfortable situation of talking to others about the power of invitations but obviously not inviting my family, and myself. I was tired, overweight, and somewhat stressed, but I had unconsciously considered that as the price one had to pay to do a first-rate job. My daughter's comment forced me to recognise my own selfishness and short-sightedness and that of many leaders like me. How can leaders expect to inspire greatness in others when they themselves are physically, emotionally and spiritually impoverished?

I learned to pace myself and attempted to create some balance in my life. It is a lifelong battle that continues, but one that is worth fighting. I thought through my priorities and organised my life accordingly. I withdrew from some voluntary activities that ate into my time. My wife and I played more golf together and took family vacations. I made sure I was home every evening for dinner even if I had an evening meeting, and generally attempted to create some balance between my home and work. A well-known Canadian radio personality, Jack Dennett, captured this idea of balance in a radio interview a few months before he passed away from cancer. He said, "I have always felt myself to be very lucky because I look forward to going to work every day, and I look forward to coming home every night."[27] (*Interview, 1975 Betty Kennedy Show*, CFBB, Toronto). As the old story goes, I have never heard of anyone on their death bed say, "I wish I had spent more time at the office."

Leaders in order to invite others must first invite themselves – *physically, intellectually, socially/emotionally, and spiritually*. As Covey has stated, private victories precede public victories.[28] There are some educational leaders who see leadership as martyrdom – "I have no choice, the job demands my total commitment". This of course is nonsense; a person always has choices. We are not Pavlovian salivating dogs. Between stimulus and response we have choices – our free will. For governments to demand that leaders motivate teachers to adopt new approaches is a disregard of a person's free will and an impossible demand. I cannot motivate or change someone else; the only one that I can change or motivate is me. I can, however, like Wayne and Garry as described in the last chapter, create a context in which people might choose to be motivated, but that takes time. Invitational leaders recognise that people have free will and chose to be engaged, motivated or supportive, and they help them to make these choices by developing a context that promotes engagement, motivation and support.

The following story of Victor Frankl reminds us that regardless of how dire our situation we always have choices. An Austrian Jew, Frankl spent the war years in a concentration camp. Like most European Jews, the Nazis had decimated his family. Yet, in the midst of a world in which everything that one holds dear was stripped from him, he described his experience:

The experiences of camp life show that man (or a woman)[29] does have a choice of action. There were enough examples, often of a heroic nature, which proved that apathy could be overcome, irritability suppressed. Man (woman) *can* preserve a vestige of spiritual freedom, of independence of mind, even in such terrible conditions of psychic and physical stress.

We who lived in the concentration camps can remember the men who walked through the huts comforting others, giving away their last piece of bread. They may have been few in number, but they offer sufficient proof that everything can be taken from a man but one thing: the last of the human freedoms – to choose one's attitude in any given set of circumstances, to choose one's own way.[30]

Inviting oneself personally is intimately linked to the second pillar of invitational leadership, inviting oneself professionally.

Inviting oneself professionally

Followers want to have confidence that their leaders know where they are going and have some idea of how to get there. To this end leaders who will succeed will assume responsibility for their own professional growth. While governments and schools assume some responsibility for the professional development of staff, true professionals retain ultimate responsibility for their own professional growth. My colleagues and I have listed elsewhere possible strategies to invite oneself professionally.[31] For convenience and to make them more memorable we have used a series of words that began with 'r'. Invitational leaders invite themselves professionally by *reading and riting* (I know it starts with w but w doesn't fit), *relating, reflecting, researching, risking* and *rehearsing*.

While these strategies are quite universal and timeless, the content of professional enrichment has changed dramatically over time. Throughout most of my career, an educational leader in Ontario could function quite nicely with a good understanding of the way education worked in Ontario and a modicum of insight into educational patterns in other provinces of Canada and the USA. Most of us had no idea what was happening in other parts of the world. It is no longer sufficient to know only that which is happening in one's local jurisdiction or even province, state or country. Just as trade, politics, and culture have gone global, so has education. Thanks to modern communications technology, educational leaders must be in tune with international trends. Ideas that took years to spread now flow freely throughout the educational world. Educators in one country can initiate ideas one day, and they can be on some policy-maker's desk half way around the world the next. Educational globalisation is alive and well and parochialism is a one way trip to insularity and regression. Each of these strategies, therefore, must be viewed through an international lens.

Reading

The last ten years have brought profound changes in educational research not only in terms of productivity but also in approach. Long-held truths have been challenged, new theories presented, and the voices of real people in real schools are finally being heard. Throughout the world there are excellent journals available to leaders. I find the *Times Educational Supplement* from the UK and *Education Week* in the USA particularly useful.

(W) 'riting'

Similarly, opportunities to write for national and international journals are available. Many journals are looking for practitioners to contribute articles on applications of research. For example, Debra Brydon[32] provides many opportunities for practitioners to share their ideas internationally on-line. For those of us who are reluctant writers (with a w), word processors make the chore less imposing. There are few better ways to sharpen thought processes and hone one's educational thinking than to commit to paper.

Relating

Relating to others through networks is a source of great support and learning. Heads' associations can provide tremendous moral and professional support. Modern means of communication make it easy to communicate with colleagues all over the world. The National College for School Leadership in England provides powerful examples of leadership networks.

Reflecting

Reflective practice as popularised by Schon[33] and others, is also a vital part of inviting oneself professionally. Reflection is the practice or art of analysing one's actions, decisions or products by focusing on our process of achieving them. Smyth[34] poses the following questions as a starting point for the reflective practitioner:

- What do I do? (reflect on one's actions)

- What does this mean? (get at the principles behind those actions)

- How did I come to be this way? (force an introspective examination of one's paradigms or mind maps)

- How might I do this differently? (re-examine the result of practice as a prerequisite to change or modification of behaviour)

To invite oneself professionally, a leader needs to answer these questions in an honest and rigorous way. Perhaps more importantly, leaders who must contend with multiple issues need to set aside time for personal reflection in order to avoid burnout. At the same time, they need to protect their colleagues from extraneous disruptions in order to preserve their psychic energy.

Researching

School and classroom research are also useful ways to invite oneself professionally. Small-scale projects to examine the efficacy of a teaching approach, or a curriculum initiative, or school-wide practices or policies are useful ways to direct or redirect practice. Action research by the school head can prepare the leader professionally to respond to the real needs of the school and not just the issues of the most vocal.

Risk taking

To invite oneself professionally one must, as Fullan[35] suggests, practise fearlessness and other forms of risk taking. Block[36] states that leadership choices are between maintenance and greatness, caution and courage, dependence and autonomy. Invitational leaders practise greatness, courage and autonomy but with discretion and preparation. Part of that preparation is to mobilise the various stakeholders in the pursuit of common goals. Invitational leaders will require a sense of timing; they will need to know when to be courageous and when to be cautious.

Rehearsing

For difficult meetings, presentations or other important activities, preparation involves rehearsing. If you have a difficult phone call from a parent or the media, ensure that someone always screens your calls and gets sufficient information about the issue or problem. Muster as much evidence or information related to that issue as you can and find someone you trust to practise your response on before you return the call at an appropriate time. Similarly, if you have an important presentation to colleagues, governors or the community, try it out first on a critical friend or coach.

It seems to me that an important part of a fulfilling and fulfilled life is continuous learning.[37] Take for example the well known principle which says that a person rises to his or her level of incompetence. The lesser known principle says that a person who was once competent and has ceased to learn and grow becomes increasingly incompetent. The well known American actress and businesswoman Jane Fonda asserts that, "everything spirals downward, rots and decays, except the human spirit, which has the capacity to grow and evolve upwards."[38] Indeed, Csikszentmihalyi[39] states that it "is not too far fetched to suggest that the growth of businesses is in large part the result of their leaders' need to grow as persons." My experiential evidence suggests that this is true of schools and school districts. Subsequent chapters in this book will have much more to say on professional growth and development.

Inviting others personally

In an information society, people carry their intellectual capital between their ears. In past times human capital meant sacrificing one's humanity to become part of a larger machine-like organisation. Humans were but another replaceable part of the larger mechanism. Taylorist management methods of predictability and control were probably necessary to get people to conform to the dictates of management. In an information-based society, however, instrumental images of people are not only dehumanising and ethically reprehensible, but also unproductive and wasteful. Leaders, especially in labour-intensive places like schools, need to relate to staff members on a personal level. This is where the core values of invitational leadership come into action:

- trust because people need to feel that risk taking is balanced by security;

- optimism because people need hope;

- respect because people need to feel cared for;

- intentionality because people need to know that they are trusted and that their efforts are for a purpose greater than themselves.[40]

The essence of the educational enterprise is its essential humanity. We are not in the business of making cars or selling bonds or constructing buildings. Our jobs are to promote pupil learning and we do that by inviting others personally to see themselves as able, worthwhile and valuable. The late United Nations Secretary General Dag Hammarskjöld wrote:

We glide past each other. But why? Why?
We reach out towards the other.
In vain – because we have never dared to give ourselves
What better thing do we have to give?[41]

Invitational leaders who invite others personally dare to give of themselves to release the energy and creativity of others. Andy Hargreaves explains this notion of releasing people's energies when he states:

In an adequate school, teachers perform to expected standards or levels of competence. In a truly effective and educationally enriching one, teachers exceed such expectations. The ability and desire to exceed expectations springs from discretionary commitment – from teachers being prepared to work above and beyond the official call of duty, entirely of their own volition. A leader who is an effective staff developer wants and knows how to create the conditions in which teachers possess that discretionary commitment. Such a leader also avoids or confronts conditions in the workplace and beyond that undermine that commitment.[42]

Inviting others professionally

Invitational leaders who have invited themselves personally and professionally and established relationships with colleagues based on optimism, respect, trust, and intentionality are now in a position to invite others professionally. To illustrate professional invitations, I have listed a few that seem to me to be common to all the contexts that I have experienced. To build on Andy Hargreaves's idea of 'releasing' colleagues' discretionary commitment, the following 'r's' and the activities associated with them are examples of ways in which leaders invite others professionally; they include *routinising, resourcing, requiring, reflecting, reframing,* and *rejoicing.*

Routinising

Have you ever got in your car, driven to work and arrived at your classroom or office and can't remember the trip? If you are like me you are probably saying "yes, most every day". It is almost like your car is on cruise control and operates itself. While change is a significant part of life in schools, many things are quite predictable. There will be new pupils, new teachers and new parents, so procedures for induction should be planned and activated. Bullying occurs in most playgrounds, always has and always will. Procedures should exist which all staff members are required to enforce. Reporting to parents, parent conferences, community council or governors' meetings and many other predictable events can be planned, scheduled and routinely run. In effect, there are a myriad of procedures and practices that must be put on 'cruise control'. People must be able not only to trust the leadership, they must be able to trust the policies, practices, and routines that are established.

Elsewhere,[43] Louise Stoll and I have used the term 'sweat the small stuff' to describe the need for leaders to attend to the small details of running an organisation in order to prevent these same issues from becoming larger issues that could get in the way of student and teacher learning. It is no accident that when new leaders turned around failing schools in England,[44] they 'sweated the small stuff' first. Most of the educational management books focus on change yet continuity is equally important. In a culture of constant change and unceasing improvement efforts, teachers become stressed and burned out. The history of innovative schools is replete with evidence of over-reaching and never taking the time to 'shift gears' to be able to concentrate on consolidating changes through effective policies and procedures. Continuity is not only important for the emotional health of teachers[45] but also vital for ongoing change efforts. Exhausted teachers make very poor change agents.

Resourcing

A key competency of instructional leaders identified by Smith and Andrews[46] was the ability of leaders to support teaching with appropriate resources. They state that strong instructional leaders have the capacity to mobilise available resources to implement policies that lead to desired outcomes. To mobilise other resources, a principal must have a good grasp of what is possible and the ability to convince potentially competing groups to work together.

Resources mean more than just materials. They include, for example, time, space, use of support staff, counselling, and advice and encouragement. In times of government cuts in all resources in the name of efficiency, leaders are challenged to find or reorganise resources to maintain the effectiveness of the learning programme.

Requiring

Theodore Sizer[47], an American educator from Brown University, in his well known book *Horace's Compromise* describes a teacher who develops a tacit agreement with his more challenging students. He acquiesces not to challenge them if they consent not to disrupt the class and bother him. Invitational leaders would find this kind of arrangement intolerable because they hold high standards for both student and teacher performance. As I suggested in Chapter 1, the commitment to student learning is the core purpose of schools and schooling and as such is not negotiable. Not only do practices like Horace's prevent learning, they dehumanise the people involved. By ignoring certain students, or overlooking unacceptable behaviours, teachers like Horace communicate the message to students that they are not very able, of little value, and incapable of achieving important 'learnings' or acting in responsible ways. One of my colleagues used to have a poster in her office that said "God don't make no junk." While the grammar is problematic, it conveys an eloquent message that 'learning centred schools are for all the students, not just academic, social, ethnic, religious, or racial elites'.

The effective schools literature is very clear: effective schools are well managed. Not only do effective schools expect, and require, positive student and teacher behaviour, they use time wisely and hold high expectations for all students. Leaders hold themselves and their followers accountable. They make sure the rules that are agreed on are enforced, that government regulations are adhered to, that the national, state or provincial curriculum is in place, that the school is prepared for inspections, and that students are ready for whatever tests they may face. We may not like some of these outside requirements, but until they change we owe it to our students to insist on meeting them.

Reflecting

Reflecting in this sense moves beyond personal reflection and suggests that invitational leaders not only reflect on their own behaviour, but that they encourage their colleagues to question their own as well as organisational policies and practices. In education, as in most other endeavours, leaders must have well-oiled, well-tuned, crap detectors. Necessity, efficiency, and urgency are the tools of technocrats and inquiry, memory, ethics, common sense, and a healthy scepticism, the guardians of the public good. There are plenty of people with answers, but few with the courage to ask the right questions. "Knowing and remembering to ask the right questions requires wisdom and judgment."[48] A significant part of the leader's job is to act as a gate-keeper, to ask the right questions, to know what initiatives to support, what to oppose, and what to subvert. A learning organisation, therefore, asks questions – questions such as:

- Who are we?

- What is our purpose?

- Is this purpose focused on student learning?

- What do we do and what do we not do to achieve this purpose?

- What do we need to learn and what do we need to unlearn to achieve our purpose?

- How do external mandates contribute to our student learning?

- Do they contribute to teacher learning?

- What do we then do about them?

Reframing

There is an old story of four blind men encountering an elephant and trying to determine what it is. One blind man feeling a leg declares the unknown object to be a tree. A second blind man feeling a tusk declares the object to be a spear, a third man holding on to a squirming trunk decides it must be a snake, and the fourth touching an ear indicates that they have found a fan. Development of improvement strategies in a school can often take on this kind of scenario. Participants identify the school's needs and directions from their unique perceptions. It is the leader's role to see the entire organisation and help stakeholders to view the school in an holistic, ecological way. To promote the holistic view leaders must learn how to look at change in multi-dimensional ways. Reframing requires participants to look at change through multiple frames or lenses,[49] before launching into solutions to problems. It requires time spent in constructive dialogue at the front of a change process that not only problem solves, but problem seeks. Without such a process, problems will emerge later on in the form of full-scale crises. Only at this point does problem solving become a destructive 'fire-fighting' process. A friend of ours belongs to a volunteer fire department in a rural area. He claims that his department has never lost a building foundation yet. Like his fire department, failure to spend the time and energy at the beginning of a change process will destroy staff collegiality and morale.

The following frames, developed with colleagues at the Ontario Institute for Studies in Education,[50] have proven very useful in helping schools to deal with the changing landscape of education in Ontario – purpose, passion or emotions, politics, structure, culture, organisational learning, leadership. The change frames model is about finding appropriate invitations within a school's unique context to invite fellow professionals to work towards positive change in schools. Let me illustrate by using the implementation of new computer technology in schools as an example of how leaders can invite others professionally using the change frames.

The purpose frame

Invitational leaders encourage staff members to talk meaningfully about the purposes of computers in the school and how they contribute to the learning of students, and work to develop a staff-wide view on this. Moreover, the leader promotes a climate in which staff members periodically review the relevance of their purposes, and evaluate the degree to which implementation of technology meets these purposes.

The passion frame

People respond emotionally to innovation. For some, technology and computers especially are rather scary. Because of their own scholarly backgrounds and experience teachers are used to directing learning in the classroom, but in the case of computer use many students are more knowledgeable than their teachers. Invitational leaders, therefore, demonstrate their understanding of the emotional aspects of change by building systems to support and empower teachers and their students to employ technology in productive ways. Simply stated, leaders ensure that the process of implementing technology actively attends to the emotions of students, teachers, and their parents.

The political frame

The implementation of a computer plan in a school often surfaces latent micro-political rivalries. Control of expensive technology means school-wide influence and power. Who should get the hardware? Where should it be located? Who is in charge? How do teachers and students access the machines? It usually falls to leaders to sort out these competing and often conflicting interests, and to ensure that people use the resources in ways that are compatible with an agreed sense of purpose. In some situations this is a tall order.

The culture frame

Invitational leaders build collaborative cultures. It becomes the leader's responsibility to develop a culture that encourages co-operation in the use of computers among teachers and students, whilst ensuring that individuals can pursue their own interests. Implementing a computer program in a school can be a useful way to promote support networks among teachers, students, and community members. The challenge of implementing computers and other technology, if handled well, has the potential to contribute to staff and student collegiality. Conversely, it can rip a school apart.

The learning frame

For most teachers, this is perhaps the most important frame. The leader ensures that staff members have regular opportunities to acquire computer literacy, reflect on the use of computers in their classrooms, work together to solve problems, and evaluate students' learning experiences continually. This suggests the need to share good practices, network with colleagues inside and outside of the school, and to stay current on appropriate software.

The leadership frame

Invitational leaders share leadership. To implement a major initiative such as computers across the curriculum, the formal leader must identify leaders across the school who can contribute to the agreed purposes. This raises questions about who makes what decisions. How do teachers and students resolve conflicts over access and usage? Who takes leadership to decide on types of hard and software? Invitational leaders share leadership, delegate effectively, and hold people accountable for their actions.

The structure frame

Leaders and their colleagues should look at the structure frame last. It answers the question of how we can create structures that advance our purposes and respond to the issues raised by the other frames. When a school's staff address structure first, all other frames must conform to pre-determined limits, and imagination and creativity are squeezed out of the discussion. Invitational leaders ensure that time and space are used in ways that provide appropriate computer access to the teachers and students who use them. Similarly, leaders ensure that roles and responsibilities are clearly delineated so that people's energies are concentrated on student learning and not micro-political issues. This requires building a staff consensus on a timetable, access, location, technical support, and in-service for teachers.

For some, the approach I have just described will be disappointing because it does not provide a step-by-step process for implementation. What it does do, however, is to assist school leaders and their colleagues to ask better questions of how computers are to be used in their unique contexts, and by using the collective wisdom of the school staff and other stakeholders to discover answers, which will enhance learning for all students. Finally, when we arrive at our destination it is time to congratulate ourselves and rejoice.

Rejoicing

One of the cultural norms of 'moving' schools is that they celebrate; they have fun.[51] Staff members enjoy the pupils and each other's company. A sure sign of the 'attrition of change' is that the exhilaration, passion, and joy of working with children and young people disappear into a 'black hole' of exhaustion, cynicism, and negativity. Invitational leaders find reasons and ways to rejoice. In a world that seems to want to confess everyone else's sins, the challenge for leaders is to seize on the positive and celebrate the victories.

Having said all this and nothing is for sure in our post-modern world, indeterminacy is a permanent part of our larger culture. There is one thing, however, of which I am sure; invitational leaders can make a difference in any situation.

Conclusion

Chapter 1 has outlined the challenges of contemporary leadership and chapters 2 and 3 have described inherently conservative aspects of educational leadership core purposes and values. Chapter 2 contends that like great businesses and other successful organisations, fundamental purposes do not change over time and that the purpose of school leadership was, is, and will be, to enhance student learning by developing student-learning centred schools. To this end, this chapter has presented a set of core values and a theory of everything that support this purpose and will persist through time, providing a platform from which leaders can evaluate and respond to their changing contexts. Paradoxically, schools like other organisations cannot and should not sit still and rest on their laurels. They need to grow and progress or suffer entropy. School leaders must balance the necessity of preserving core purposes and values with the equally compelling obligation to engage all their key stakeholders to adapt to new contextual circumstances. They must involve staff, students and parents in discovering ways to invent different approaches to existing problems, to abandon dated practices, experiment with new ideas, imagine alternative futures, create engaging learning experiences for all students, and develop their school's capacity to anticipate and deal with change. The chapters that follow take up this challenge to look at how educational systems can develop and sustain leaders who must address this complexity while balancing the forces of continuity and change. As a preliminary step, Chapter 4 describes and explains the nature of the intellectual qualities that all of us mere mortals possess, and the importance of developing these to develop and sustain educational leaders.

Notes

1   Purkey, W.W. and Novak, J.M. (1996). *Inviting School Success: A self-concept theory approach to teaching and learning, and democratic practice*, 3rd edition. Belmont, CA: Wadsworth.
2   Purkey, W.W. and Strahan, D. 'School transformation through invitational education', *Research in the Schools*, 2 (2): pp. 1–6.
3   Quoted in Csikszentmihalyi, M. (2004). *Good Business: Leadership, flow, and the making of meaning.* New York: Penguin Books.
4   Stoll and Fink (1996) op. cit.
5   Mintzberg, H. (2004). *Managers not MBAs: A hard look at the soft practice of managing and management development.* San Francisco, CA: Berrett-Koehler, p. 144.
6   Kouzes, J.M. and Posner, B.Z. (2003). *Credibility: How leaders gain and lose it, why people demand it.* San Francisco, CA: Jossey-Bass, p. 5.

7   Williams, P. (2002). *The Paradox of Power.* New York: Warner/Faith, p. 88.

8   Kouzes, J.M. and Posner, B.Z. (2003). 'Leadership is a relationship', in *Business Leadership: A Jossey-Bass Reader.* San Francisco, CA: Jossey-Bass, p. 253.

9   Ibid, p. 252.

10 See Malloy, K. (1998). *Building a learning community: The story of New York City Community School District #2.* Pittsburg, PA: Learning Research and Development Centre, University of Pittsburg; Newman, F.M. & Associates (1996) *Authentic Achievement: restructuring schools for intellectual quality.* San Francisco, CA: Jossey-Bass; Louis, K.S-. and Kruse, S.D. (eds) (1996) *Professionalism and Community Perspectives on Reforming Urban Schools.* Thousand Oaks, CA: Corwin Press; Meier, D. (1995) *The Power of Their Ideas: Lessons from America from a small school in Harlem.* Boston, MA: Beacon Press.

11 Bennis, W. (2000). *Managing the Dream: Reflections on leadership and change.* Cambridge, MA: Perseus Publishing, p. 21.

12 Bryk, A.S. and Schneider, B. (2003). 'Trust in schools: Core resource for school reform', *Educational Leadership,* 60 (6): p. 42.

13 Kouzes and Posner (2003) op. cit., p. 19.

14 Covey, S. (1989). *The 7 Habits of Highly Effective People: Powerful lessons in personal change.* New York: Simon and Schuster.

15 Quoted in Williams (2002) op. cit., pp. 87–9.

16 Since a middle school mathematics teacher was paid a lower salary than an assistant principal, 'grandfathering' meant that the school district would maintain his assistant principal's salary until the salary for a middle school teacher with his qualifications caught up. In other words, he would not lose any money.

17 Glasser, W.W. (1997). 'A new look at school failure and school success', *Phi Delta Kappa,* 78 (8): 596–602.

18 Giuliani, R. (2002). *Leadership.* op. cit., p. 298.

19 Kouzes and Posner (2003) op. cit.

20 Goleman, D., Boyatzis, R. and McKee, A. (2003). 'Primal Leadership', in *Business Leadership: A Jossey-Bass Reader.* San Francisco, CA: Jossey-Bass, p. 53.

21 Sergiovanni, T. (2004). 'Building a community of hope', *Educational Leadership,* 61 (8): pp. 33–7.

22 Csikszentmihalyi, M. (2004). *Good Business: Leadership, flow, and the making of meaning.* New York: Penguin Books. p. 4.

23 Purkey and Novak, op. cit.

24 Collins, J.C. and Porras, J.I. (1994). *Built to Last.* New York: Harper Business Essentials, pp. 201–2.

25 For greater insight into invitational theory and practice see Purkey, W.W. and Novak, J.M. (1996) *Inviting School Success: A self-concept theory approach to teaching and learning, and democratic practice.* 3rd

edition. Belmont, CA: Wadsworth; Purkey, W.W. and Siegel, B. (2003) *Becoming an Invitational Leader: A new approach to professional and personal success*. Atlanta, GA: Humanics Trade Group; Novak, J. (2002) *Inviting Educational leadership: Fulfilling potential and applying an ethical perspective to the educational process*. London: Pearson Education. My own work on the topic is in Stoll and Fink (1996) op. cit., and Stoll, Fink and Earl (2003) op. cit.

26 Covey, S. (1973) Presentation for the Halton Board of Education.
27 Betty Kennedy Show (1975) Interview, CFRB, Toronto.
28 Covey, S. (1989). *The 7 Habits of Highly Effective People: Powerful Lessons in Personal Change*. New York: Simon and Schuster, p. 51.
29 My edit.
30 Frankl, V.E. (1984). *Man's Search for Meaning*. New York: Washington Square Press, p. 89.
31 Stoll, Fink and Earl (2003) op. cit.
32 Check the following website – www.icponline.org or contact Debra directly at brydon@bigpond.net.au.
33 Schon, D. (1987). *Educating the Reflective Practitioner*. San Francisco, CA: Jossey Bass.
34 Smyth, J. (1989). 'Developing and Sustaining Critical Reflection in Teacher Education', *Journal of Teachers Education*, 40 (2): pp. 2–9.
35 Fullan, M.G. (1991). *The New Meaning of Educational Change*. New York: Teachers' College Press, p. 167.
36 Block, P. (1991). *The Empowered Manager*. San Francisco, CA: Jossey Bass.
37 I received my PhD at the age of 60, and completed three books between the ages of 60 and 65.
38 Quoted in Csikszentmihalyi, M. (2004) *Good Business: Leadership, flow, and the making of meaning*. New York: Penguin Books, p. 35.
39 Csikszentmihalyi, M. (2004). Ibid. p. 64.
40 Fullan, M.G. (1993). *Change Forces: Probing the depths of educational reform*. London: Falmer Press.
41 Hammarskjöld, D. (1963). *Markings*. New York: Alfred A. Knopf Ltd, p. 40.
42 Hargreaves, A. (1998). 'The emotional politics of teaching and teacher development: with implications for educational leadership', *International Journal for Leadership in Education*, 1 (4): 316–36, 314.
43 Stoll and Fink (1996) op. cit.
44 National Commission on Education (1996). *Success Against the Odds*. London: Routledge; Stoll, L. and Myers, K. (eds) (1998). *Schools in Difficulty: No quick fixes*. London: Falmer Press.
45 Hargreaves (1998) op. cit.
46 Smith, W.F. and Andrews, R.L. (1989). *Instructional Leadership: How principals make a difference*. Alexandria, VA: Association for Supervision and Curriculum Development, p. 11.

47 Sizer, T. (1992). *Horace's Compromise*. New York: Houghton Mifflin.

48 Secretan, L.H. (1996). *Reclaiming the Higher Ground: Creating organizations that inspire the soul*. Toronto, ON: Macmillan, p. 4.

49 Boleman, L. and Deal, T. (1997). *Reframing Organizations*: *Artistry, choice and leadership* (2nd Edition) San Francisco, CA: Jossey-Bass; Fink, D. (2000). op.cit; Louis, K., Toole, J. and Hargreaves, A. (1999). 'Rethinking school improvement', in Louis, K., Toole, J. and Hargreaves, A. (eds), *Handbook of Research in Education Administration*. New York: Longman, pp. 251–76.

50 Hargreaves, A., Shaw, P., Fink, D., Retallick, J., Giles, C., Moore, S., Schmidt, M. and James-Wilson, S. (2000) *Change Frames: Supporting secondary teachers in interpreting and integrating secondary school reform*. Toronto, ON: Ontario Institute for Studies in Education/University of Toronto.

51 Stoll and Fink (1996) op. cit.

4   *Qualities*

Mihaly Csikszentmihalyi[1] employs the metaphor of 'flow' to describe optimal experience. A person can be seen to be in 'flow' when goals are clear and immediate and relevant feedback is provided, and when a person's skills are completely engaged in overcoming a particular challenge that is just about manageable. Athletes will often talk about being 'in a zone'. Musicians in 'flow' seem enraptured. We have all experienced the enjoyment and productivity of 'flow' – perhaps when you mastered that particularly difficult piano concerto, or finally broke 80 on the golf course, or taught an outstanding lesson, or handled that politically demanding meeting with skill and efficiency. For leaders, facing the complexity of educational change in the twenty first century the challenges are formidable, but so is our potential to develop the skills or abilities to reach a condition of 'flow' in which one remains focused on the task, but happy in the process.

The first step is to disabuse ourselves of the mythology of heroic leadership which suggests that only a few unique and 'chosen' people can become great leaders. Like Dorothy in *The Wizard of Oz* who pulls back the curtain and finds that the wizard isn't really a wizard but a normal human being, we need to recognise that great or outstanding educational leaders are not heroic or larger than life but mere mortals. Collins and Porras[2] report that the CEOs of the great companies "are not necessarily more brilliant, more charismatic, more creative, more complex thinkers, more adept at coming up with great ideas – in short, more wizardlike – than the rest of us." What these corporate leaders have done, however, is to develop, exercise and employ their innate abilities or 'qualities' persistently, cohesively, and pervasively in the performance of their role. This chapter makes the same argument about outstanding educational leaders, and in particular describes the inherent qualities that we all possess.

In evolutionary terms human survival has required us to become more complex than any other organism on the planet. Humans with their big brains have differentiated themselves from other organisms by developing their intellectual abilities, while at the same time integrating with other humans to create complex systems, societies, nations, and international organisations. "The more complex a system gets to be, the more improbable it becomes, the more things can go wrong with it, and the more effort it takes to keep it from decaying."[3] For example, the concentration of our commercial, transportation and technological infrastructures in large complex cities make them attractive targets for terrorists. The education of our young people has also become increasingly complex and potentially fragile because it involves the complicated integration of governments at different levels with networks of teachers, parents and students, a multiplicity of stakeholder organisations, and innumerable private enterprises like text book publishers that depend on education for survival. To thrive within this complexity, leaders must develop their processes of differentiation and integration. Differentiation involves "realizing that we are unique individuals, responsible for our own survival and well-being, who are willing to develop this uniqueness wherever it leads, while enjoying the expression of our being in action." The second process, integration, is the realisation that "however unique we are, we are also completely enmeshed in networks with other human beings, with cultural symbols and artefacts, and with the surrounding natural environment." A person who is more fully differentiated and integrated becomes a complex individual and "has the best chance at leading a happy, vital, and meaningful life".[4]

It is the job of educators to develop these two processes simultaneously and address the on-going tension between the promotion of individuality and release of the learning potential within an integrated social setting. In simple terms, educational leaders face the dilemma on a daily basis of balancing the demands of individuals' differentiation with the requirements of a civil society, or integration. This chapter and the next will deal with differentiation – the 'qualities' leaders need to develop, and the 'learnings' they require to achieve a state of 'flow' in which their abilities and knowledge enable them to make the challenges of educational change manageable and even enjoyable. Chapter 6 addresses integration and the trajectories educational leaders experience as they evolve in their capacity to relate and influence complex educational networks like schools and districts – but first, I will examine the 'intellectual' qualities.

The tool kit

What makes us unique as humans is our ability to consider and to make choices. As I have argued in the previous chapter, between stimulus and response humans can make choices – we have free will. We have the ability to shape events in our lives as opposed to being shaped by circumstances. The key word is ability. We may or may not use it, or circumstances may be so overwhelming that our ability is unequal to the challenge, but "to embrace this ability we need tools – qualities – which allow us to free ourselves from our own psychodrama at least long enough to consider real questions in real contexts."[5] John Ralston Saul, Canada's foremost contemporary philosopher, has identified six interrelated 'qualities' or tools that we all possess individually and collectively. These are reason, ethics, imagination, intuition, memory, and common sense.

In his book *On Equilibrium* he argues that we can learn to use each of our qualities simultaneously and effortlessly. "We can normalize the use of them so that much of the time we hardly need to stop in order to consider," and through these qualities we "can shape and direct our talents and characteristics – both ours and societies'."[6] Each of these qualities, he explains "takes its meaning from the other – from the tension in which they exist with each other."[7] In isolation, they can become distorted. Ethics can become fanaticism, reason can become irrationality, imagination can become fantasy, memory can become nostalgia, intuition can become superstition, and common sense can become nonsense. Together and 'in equilibrium' they are powerful, isolated they become distorted into ideology. "After all ideology is the easiest mechanism for leading the way. Why? Because it makes the large world small. And seemingly certain."[8]

Reason

For the most part educational literature and management programmes perseverate on the primacy of reason over other ways of knowing. Not reason as thought and argument but rather instrumental reason that is concerned with form, function and measurement. By aligning what teachers teach, how they teach it and how we know they have taught it, technocrats have elevated reason and rationality to a moral principle when it is merely a "disinterested administrative method."[9] The search for best practice and the cult of evidence-based decision making that reduce people to numbers and ignore the non-rational aspects of education reflect an ideological rather than a pragmatic stance. Ex-mayor Giuliani of New York contends that "important, complicated decisions require both statistical analysis and intuition. Statistics can provide the necessary data, but unless you apply your own intuition, gathered from your own experience, you are just a computer spitting out formulas."[10] Reason, as the all-inclusive quality, is pure ideology.

For example, fascist states were built on instrumental reason. Albert Speer, Hitler's henchman responsible for munitions and armaments, was the perfect rational technocrat who valued the technical over social and human systems. As a former architect, he very rationally employed thousands of enslaved Jews, Russians, and other Nazi captives in his armament plants. He was very efficient and very effective in his job. From his ideological perspective his actions were logical, reasonable and rational, but quite unethical, indeed reprehensible by any ethical standards of morality. As Saul comments, "logic is the art of going wrong with confidence" (2001: 124). Robert McNamara, the American Secretary of Defence, who used enemy body counts to convince Americans that they were winning the Vietnam War, initiated an arms race that has spread terror internationally. He 'very rationally' thought that the USA could produce more armaments than they needed, and use the profits of sales to friends like Iran and Iraq to defray the costs of production. Of course, the British then jumped on board and sold arms to their friends, and the French to theirs, and the Russians to theirs and so on, with little thought given to the long-term consequences, and less thought to the ethical dimensions of arms trading.

This addiction to instrumental reason and rationality has created an educational environment of structures, measurements, targets, and compliance and the search for best practice that implies there is one 'best' way to do something. As Collins and Porras[11] indicate "The real question to ask is not 'Is this practice good?' but 'Is this practice *appro-*

priate for us – does it fit with our ideology and ambitions?' "What makes instrumental reason (utilitarian, instrumental logic) so profoundly irrational is its devotion to mechanistic solutions conceived in a limited time and space, as if the matter at hand were free standing. Instrumental reason *is*[12] only because we believe it to be a form of thought, when all we are dealing with is narrow logic built from within."[13] Reason unlimited by other qualities will become irrational because everything is related to everything else. Our central protection against irrationality, therefore, is the tension between reason and our other qualities. While problem solving and data analysis strategies should play an important part in any leadership development program, they need to be presented within a context of the other intellectual qualities. The following episode illustrates the need to marry reason and rationality with the other qualities.

One of the most challenging problems that I faced as a senior educational leader was to 'rationalise our accommodations' in an area I supervised. Translated, this meant the closing of some schools. The demographics of our district had shifted requiring the creation of student accommodation in newer growth areas, and the reduction of space in more settled communities where school enrolment was in decline. The government of Ontario allowed school districts to use the money from schools they closed to open new schools in other areas. I was, therefore, asked by our school board to reduce the student spaces in a geographic area by approximately 40 per cent. From a purely rational point of view this was a fairly easy task. Just divide the number of students into the spaces available and figure out a way to eliminate the excess – a 'no brainer'. School consolidation, however, is not a purely rational activity. How people respond to potential school closures has little to do with mathematics and logic. The loss of a school can mean the extinction of a small community, particularly in rural settings. The local school also may evoke nostalgia and the loss of tradition among former students. To some in a community, a school's closure may mean the loss of jobs, influence, or engagements. Parents may fear for their children's safety in moving to other schools, or their loss of identity in larger less personal schools. Teachers and principals can also become apprehensive about their futures and subtly influence community reactions.

I understood all of this because I had had the opportunity to observe colleagues attempt to consolidate schools in another region by 'brute sanity'. They presented a group of parent representatives from each of the schools involved with a carefully worked out solution to the accommodation problems in the area, that on paper was very cleverly constructed and difficult to refute, especially since the parents on the committee lacked the expertise required in such matters. My colleagues saw their task as a 'sales job', not a legitimate community problem-solving opportunity. Once they went public with their recommendations, the backlash was immediate, voluble and emotionally charged. What was intended to be a quick, rational solution to a fairly straightforward problem became a seemingly endless series of meetings, confrontations, compromises, and eventual retreat.

When I was presented with a similar problem I was determined to do it differently. I wasn't quite sure how, but I knew I wanted to ensure enhanced learning opportunities for students, and to operate within my 'invitational' principles of trust, optimism, respect, and intentionality. Once the parental committee of two parents from each of the five schools involved had been assembled, I spent a great deal of time listening. I asked each one, what is it you would like to see happen as a result of this process? From this discussion, the committee eventually arrived at a goal statement that focused on creating a solution that produced optimum learning opportunities for all the students of all the schools. Then I asked what would it look like when we got there? These questions produced a list of criteria that ranged from proper facilities, through safety issues, to program variety and flexibility. We ended up with ten criteria. I then asked participants to weight each criterion in importance out of ten, so that program flexibility might be ten, safety seven, facilities five, and so on. At this point I invited the committee members to go back to their school communities and with the help of their school's principal, who collectively acted as non-voting advisors to the committee, to invite each school community to suggest possible school configurations that would meet our goals and criteria. We received 23 submissions. Using our weighting system, we evaluated each submission individually and collectively. This took over two months of meetings every Tuesday night. There was a great deal of thought and a lot of arguments. Timing was everything. To move too quickly was to invite criticism of forcing a solution.

Throughout the process, I did what I had learned from my colleague Wayne, and withheld my opinions and continually probed to clarify ideas, expose contradictions, and advance the process. Once we had our 23 alternatives down to three scenarios that we could all live with, we went public in a large meeting of over 500 parents and interested community members. The committee members did the talking, and explained the advantages and disadvantages as they saw them of each alternative. We then invited community members to meet with us, and present alternatives. We had agreed beforehand that we would meet until everyone who wanted to offer an alternative had had a good hearing. A few took advantage of the offer and I made sure they had all the relevant data in advance. We met for most of one full Saturday to hear various points of view. We found the presentations helpful because some contributed ideas that we had not considered, and these ideas helped to shape our final recommendations. What could have become a series of acrimonious confrontations was almost pleasant. Every delegation acknowledged our dilemma, and entered into the process in a spirit of community problem solving. It soon became clear that one of our scenarios had little public support. This left us with two. Once again through thought and argument we blended the two into one and arrived at a solution that we could take forward to the school board with unanimity and some pride. After over five months of work, the district school board unanimously approved the committee's report that recommended the closure of two of the five schools. What was most gratifying for all of us was that unlike previous consolidation efforts, not one delegation from the community opposed our recommendations.

As this vignette suggests, process is as important as product. By taking the time before arriving at a solution to engage in thought and argument, the committee avoided spending that time as others had done in acrimonious and often purposeless confrontations with the community, that left a legacy of distrust directed towards the school district and its officials. This situation further indicates that a rational process whilst important, and based on volumes of data on enrolment projections and school accommodation, must be balanced by other qualities. To illustrate, I will use this story in each of the following discussions of the qualities or 'tools' in our 'tool kits'.

Ethics

Reason unbalanced by ethics has produced holocausts, arms races and genocide. Ethics answers the question, how should I live, given the context of the larger good? "The larger good assumes the existence of the *other*, of the family, of the community. Of the public good."[14] Bishop Desmond Tutu expressed this concept well when he stated, "I am human because you are human." This is in stark contrast to the Enlightenment credo of Descartes, "I think therefore I am." Adam Smith said "The wise and virtuous man is at all times willing that his own private interest should be sacrificed to the public interest."[15] Ethics in general refers to well-based standards of right and wrong that impose reasonable obligations such as refraining from murder, stealing and assault, and promote such virtues as honesty, compassion and loyalty. Ethics also applies to standards relating to rights such as the right to life and privacy.

In education, Starratt[16] suggests that a fully-formed ethical consciousness will contain themes of caring, justice, and reflection on our values and behaviours. Schools are moral places designed to promote certain social norms and to discourage others. School leaders often face ethical dilemmas that require them to choose between two 'rights'. Do I spend the money on the program for the gifted that would be politically popular, or on programs for our mentally challenged students? Do I encourage the streaming or tracking (banding) of students that would certainly please the parents of the high achievers and many of the teachers, or construct heterogeneous classes? Do I allow meetings of religious groups in the school and risk community unrest related to some fringe groups, or ban all religious groups? Do I spend the athletic budget on a football team that involves 30 boys but promotes school spirit and community engagement, or distribute it in ways that involve all students? The list is endless. Scholars[17] tend to agree that a leader's first step must be to reflect on their own values and then strive to understand the values orientation of others. Kidder[18] suggests four broad strategies to address ethical dilemmas.

1 Leaders should have a definite sense of ethical standards and must be willing to act on this. In Chapter 3 I introduced the values of trust that promotes honesty, respect that encourages caring and justice, optimism that implies hope, and intentionality that encourages integrity in word and deed. I suggest these

values are a good starting point.

2   Leaders can examine dilemmas from different perspectives and use one of three approaches:

  • Examine the issue in the light of possible consequences of each choice and determine who will be affected and in what ways.

  • Examine the choices against well-accepted moral rules.

  • Look at the choices using the 'golden rule'. How would I like to be treated under similar circumstances?

3   Leaders can often reframe the ethical issue by looking for alternatives and avoiding 'either/or' thinking. Sometimes 'and/both' thinking can work to resolve ethical dilemmas.

4   Leaders should have the habit of conscious reflection wherever it may lead them. If leaders start from a very committed focus on learning for *all* students, and a value system built around the invitational model, leaders will possess a personal stance or reference point from which to determine their best course of action.

Each of these approaches needs to be balanced by the other qualities, or ethical solutions could easily slip into extremism – "good intentions are converted into misplaced certainty as to moral rectitude. This certainty convinces the holder of truth that he has the right to harm others."[19] Ethics can lead to fanaticism when extreme ethical positions replace normal behaviour in normal times and are not balanced by reason (as thought and argument) and common sense. Religious cults and the Taliban in Afghanistan are but two examples.

In the example of the school closure process described previously our committee faced a number of ethical issues. The most difficult involved a division in our group and in the community between schools in more affluent areas with well-organised and well-financed parents' groups, and a less cohesive working-class community in which the parents and the community were less involved in their children's schools. By defining the goal and criteria at the beginning and developing a rational problem-solving process that involved plenty of thought and argument as well as imagination, intuition and common sense, the committee's solution closed one of the middle-class schools and one of the schools in the working-class area. This recommendation took courage on the part of the committee, particularly those representatives of the middle-class schools who faced considerable pressure from their neighbours to close only the working-class schools to save their respective schools. The representatives of the middle-class schools never wavered because they felt the process had resulted in a just resolution of the issue, and they had grounded their decisions on a strong ethical principle – quality education for *all* the children of the community. By taking plenty of time and following a democratic process, all the delegates believed that we had arrived at a common-sense solution.

Common sense

Common sense is shared knowledge that carries us above self-interest. "Shared knowledge by its very nature is a consideration of the whole. It is essentially inclusive and human"[20] and provides a shortcut to making decisions very quickly. If we depend on pure reason and logic for every decision we make we would accomplish very little. Common sense, however,

> knows how to draw conclusions even in the face of incomplete or unreliable information ... Common sense knows how to deal with a problem that is so complex it cannot even be specified. Common sense knows how to revise beliefs based on facts that all of a sudden are proved false. Logic was not built for any of these scenarios.[21]

Saul argues that there are two forms of common sense – shared knowledge within society (e.g. education is important) versus superstitions or truths (e.g. private is always superior to public) that are declared to be visible, evident and inevitable. These two versions of common sense are continually at war and "so long as we accept the idea of self-evident and therefore inevitable truth – for example, that we are driven by self interest or technology leads society – our passivity will prepare us for ideological manipulation."[22] In Ontario, we experienced the so-called 'common-sense revolution' that cut public services to the core and gave huge tax breaks to the wealthy. For those who worked in schools, hospitals and social agencies it was pure ideology and destructive nonsense, but for the true believers it was self-evident truth and 'common sense'. Common sense, therefore, is also the easiest of the qualities to deform into nonsense. Pretence of simplicity and truth can easily be presented as self-evident truth.

For example, if students are attending school they have a much better chance of learning the state's curriculum; this is common sense. Since the exclusion from school of some students makes life easier for teachers and principals, some would argue that exclusion is in everyone's best interest, and therefore common sense. This line of reasoning is an example of 'conventional wisdom' or at least unexamined practice that has become false common sense designed to ensure the passivity of others. Similarly, practices like tracking, age-grade organisations, subject based curriculum, standardised tests, to name but a few examples of the "grammar of schooling,"[23] have remained largely unchallenged and unchanged for years and have become part of what some might consider the common-sense way to organise education.

In my experience, I have observed some leaders who seemed to have good common sense and others who seemed to lack it. The difference it seems to me was in the quality of their judgements in any given situation. Some seemed to be able to defuse potentially difficult situations effortlessly, and move them on to resolution with apparent ease. Others could turn a minor issue into a crisis in 15 minutes. Those who appeared to act with common sense had developed a well thought out philosophy of leadership based on a clear sense of purpose and a firm set of values that seemed to guide their actions. They had also acquired inviting interpersonal skills and had learned problem-solving processes that enabled them to turn potentially difficult situations into constructive ones. They seemed almost intuitively to read the situation and respond appropriately. Their common sense appeared to have within it an "instinct" or "special feeling" for the truth.[24] The two examples that follow illustrate the complexity of what we know as common sense.

Examples

The elected officials in my school district where I spent most of my career decided that the area superintendent[25] for each school had to approve all school trips. As principal, this process really bothered me because I thought I was the best person after the relevant teacher involved to judge the educational efficacy of a school trip, and in practice my supervisor automatically approved my recommendations anyway. When I became an area superintendent, however, one of the principals who reported to me sent a school trip proposal to me for my approval, expecting it to be 'rubber stamped'. To the principal's surprise, I turned it down because my common sense told me, "this is too risky."

The trip involved a well-regarded, unmarried, male teacher who had, over a number of years, loaded up his van (people mover) with his 12 and 13 year old students on weekends and taken them on educationally related trips. I felt that in light of the potential for an accusation of sexual abuse that this was a 'dodgy' practice for a single male teacher, with students of both genders. Frankly, there was no evidence of any problems in the past, and the students and their parents generally supported these trips. I said I would approve if they could find a female chaperone to go along. Since the teacher would not accommodate my requirement, the trips came to an end. What I thought was common sense had within it a fair amount of intuition – the situation just didn't look and feel right. Needless to say I had an upset teacher, principal, and not a few students and parents. Ironically, a few years later the same teacher was convicted of sexual abuse stemming from episodes earlier in his career and thus lost his teaching licence. Certainly, my notion of common sense differed greatly from the principal's and the teacher's and resulted in different judgements on the same situation. I suspect I had unconsciously melded my intuition with my experience or 'memory' and employed some reason and logic and my ethical principles to make my judgement. As it turned out my instincts were right, in this situation, but my idea of common sense could have just as easily been wrong.

The second example I can draw on occurred within the school consolidation committee that I described earlier. As I indicated we had three alternatives that we took to public meeting. One recommended integrating 12 and 13 year old students (grades 7 and 8)[26] into a local secondary school that had superb facilities and a fair amount of room available. The arguments for this alternative were compelling. In addition to facilities, our school district had a successful example of a school that enrolled students from 12 to 17 years of age, and of course we referred to the pattern in other countries such as England where students enter secondary school at 11 or 12 years of age. It became very clear to the committee, however, from the public meeting and the community feedback sessions that enacting this alternative would have unleashed a tremendous community backlash. The committee unanimously decided that it was only common sense to eliminate the secondary school as an alternative. From the perspective of the community as a whole, this decision made very good sense, but from a purely rational, logical perspective it could be viewed a political expediency and lacking in 'common sense'. This decision made the need for an imaginative solution to our dilemma even more crucial.

Imagination

Rolf Jensen, of the Copenhagen Institute for Future Studies has suggested that:

> We are in the twilight of a society based on data. As information and intelligence become the domain of computers, society will place new value on the one human ability that can't be automated: emotion. Imagination, myth, ritual – the language of emotion – will affect everything from our purchasing decisions to how well we work with others ... Companies will thrive on the basis of their stories and myths. Companies will need to understand that their products are less important than their stories.[27]

If this is true in business then it seems to follow that in an age of creativity, educators need to free themselves and others from the bonds of conformity, control and compliance. Leaders of learning must not only release their own abilities to imagine, but also must create a rich stimulating context in which their colleagues can develop their imaginations to create and innovate. Leaders do not necessarily have to generate imaginative solutions to complex problems that our schools face, but they must be able to recognise and act on creative ideas that emerge from others. Imagination is the quality that allows us to picture a 'realistic' future because it most naturally draws all our qualities together. It protects us from premature conclusions – "just when we think we understand, it leaps ahead again into more uncertainty. And so imagination is naturally inclusive and inconclusive" and "Imagination is our primary force for progress because it is driven by ideas – incomplete, aggressive, inconclusive ideas."[28] Saul contends that policies can only survive if they continue to be led by ideas – by the imagination. "The moment the direction slips into managerial logic, they begin to fall apart, because they are no longer linked directly to the reality and the collective unconscious of society."[29] As he explains:

> Those who believe in the dominance of understanding and methodology seem to miss the obvious. The tools they consider marginal – those of the arts – are in fact the tools of story telling and reimagining ourselves, which all humans use. And why do we use them? In order to convince ourselves that we exist as humans and as individuals in a society.[30]

Imagination in schools or districts is more than just extrapolating from existing circumstances and developing alternative scenarios, but rather it is looking for discontinuities. The "goal is less to understand the future than to understand the revolutionary portent in what is *already* changing. To look for things where the *rate of change*[31] is changing – for inflection points that foreshadow significant discontinuities."[32] To illustrate, I have modified the following questions posed by Hamel for 'potential business revolutionaries' to fit educational contexts:

- Where and in what ways is change creating the potential for new rules and new opportunities? If something isn't expressly forbidden then the door is open to action. Remember it is easier to get forgiveness than permission.

- What is the potential for revolution (or at least significant change) inherent in the things that are changing *right now*, or have *already* changed? For example, the British government has initiated discussions with the British educational community on 'personalised learning'. This view of education suggests that schools need to respond to the unique needs of each student. This is in contrast to the existing paradigm of schools that obliges students to conform to the schools' pre-existing practices and structures. If this paradigm shift sounds familiar, it is exactly what Lord Byron was about in 1970 (see Chapter 2). I suspect most politicians who talk about the concept have not figured out its revolutionary potential, but it provides wonderful opportunities for imaginative British educators to move that nation's education system even more into an age of creativity.

- What are the discontinuities? Perhaps the most fundamental is the 'two solitudes' between policy makers and policy implementers. As Chapter 1 suggests, the standards/standardisation agenda is based upon predictability, control and compliance, while our society and economy cry out for creativity, entrepreneurialism and flexibility. The opportunities are in the spaces within this paradox.[33]

- Which aspects of what is changing can we come to know better than anyone else in our educational community does? What does your district or school do really well, or what could you learn to do really well, in fact, better than any other school district or school? What is there in which your district or school could be 'world-class' (remember you are now global educators whether you like it or not)?

- What is the deep dynamic that will make our new educational concept oh-so-relevant right now? For example, if you are a British educator operating in an environment where people are talking about 'personalised learning' what aspect of it can you address immediately? For American educators, the question might be; how could we promote 'deep' learning for our students while meeting the requirements of No Child Left Behind? How can we make the rhetoric of the legislation a reality?

Imagination unlocks our creativity but it also requires us to develop our inner resources. Imagination and creativity involve

not only a passionate interest but a self confidence too. A person needs a healthy self respect to pursue novel ideas, and to make mistakes despite criticism from others. Self doubt there may be, but it cannot always win the day. Breaking generally accepted rules, or even stretching them, takes confidence. Continuing to do so in the face of scepticism and scorn, takes even more.[34]

At the same time leaders will have to be mindful that imagination without the context of the other qualities can lead to fantasy. The following two vignettes illustrate the use of imagination and its connections to the other qualities.

Example

During my tenure as principal, our school moved from an old building into a new facility. It was an exciting and stressful time as I tried to run a school, while chairing a new school design committee, and organising the move. One of my staff members came to me and said that he had an idea for the cafeteria in the new school. He said why don't we run it and use it as an extension of our programs, and make use of any profits to benefit the school? At the time this was a wild idea because the district contracted the operation of all school cafeterias to an outside company and pocketed some of the profits. The quality of cafeteria food in most schools, however, was a subject of some rather dark humour. I liked the idea of our school running the cafeteria because it could be sold educationally on the basis of linking the operation of the cafeteria to our accounting and business programs as well as home economics. Besides if we operated it, we could hire our own students who needed to make a little money.

The idea was the easy part. The district business department found a million reasons why it wouldn't work, but fortunately I was able to convince one of the more influential district business people that it was an idea worth pursuing. Together we developed a detailed plan with all the possible facts and figures anyone could ever want, and took it forward. When the new school opened, we had our cafeteria staff in place and conducted the cafeteria as an extension of the learning facilities. We offered lower priced, more wholesome food than any other school in the district, and made a considerable profit that at the time went towards the purchase of computers. Our success ultimately obliged the district to change its policies for operating the cafeterias in the district so that other schools could follow our lead.

A few years later after I had became an area superintendent, two of Lord Byron's most outstanding teachers came to me with an idea that they had tried to get off the ground with little success. They proposed the creation of a school for people who had left school without a graduation diploma and needed flexible hours to balance school with their jobs. They suggested a school that opened at 7:00 in the morning and closed at 9:00 or 10:00 at night. Programs would be individualised or in small groups and taught by a small cadre of versatile, innovative teachers. This 'Self Reliant' centre needed money, space, equipment and system support. Since I thought it was an excellent idea and ahead of its time, I put together a proposal with the help of many colleagues and took it forward to the senior leaders of the system. They liked the idea but advised that they thought that the elected politicians would object to the amount of money it required. I redrafted the plan to begin the project as a small pilot program and then to build it from there.

My theory, borrowed from Michael Fullan, was to start small but keep thinking big. This plan was approved, but unfortunately my two idealistic initiators felt it was so 'watered down' they wanted nothing to do with it. The program met an immediate need in the community and over the next three years it kept growing until it had spread to other regions of the district and it continues to thrive to this day. Interestingly, four years after the initial pilot began, one of the initiators joined the program as a teacher whilst the other left education to become one of the region's top child psychiatrists, but he still keeps a close eye on his brainchild.

These two stories illustrate the notion that leaders need not initiate the great ideas but they need to recognise them when they appear. In both cases, I was told by other principals and senior officials that the projects defied common sense, that I was impractical, "rocking the boat" and a "wide-eyed idealist." Fortunately, I had reason and logic on my side and the support of some influential people in the district. With their help I was very well prepared. One the former mayor of New York's principles of leadership is to "prepare, prepare, prepare." As Rudolf Giuliani states "no one, no matter how gifted, can perform without careful preparation, thoughtful experiment, and determined follow-through."[35] By combining other people's imaginative ideas with my careful preparation and knowledge of the school district, and an instinct for knowing when and from whom to seek support, both situations proved highly successful. I wish I could say that about all my creative projects. I could tell you how my proposal to run a school without a building, but just buses to move students and teacher around the community so that we could conduct a truly experiential school, crashed and burned on takeoff, but that's for another book.

Intuition

Wayne Gretzky is generally considered to be the finest ice hockey player in the history of the game. When asked to explain his excellence he replied, "you must skate to where the puck is going, not where it is."[36] His intuition was the product of his experience, his imagination and his obvious talent. Like other great athletes in 'flow', he could slow the play down in his mind and see the entire ice surface and the location of the other players. In a similar vein, the renowned founder of polio vaccination Jonas Salk suggested that intuition is when the intuitive mind tells the logical mind where to go next. By talking and watching people in high-stress, high-risk jobs like fire-fighting, nursing, and emergency medicine, Klein[37] discovered these people did not ask "what do I do", when confronted by an emergency, but rather they intuitively asked, "what is happening here"? By reading the cues and patterns they determined from the environment they moved to action. This is quite the opposite of rational problem solving in which decision makers develop a range of alternatives and based on the evidence choose the best solution. In a crisis this would be folly. For example, once fire fighters decide on a course of action, they quickly imagine the results of that action, and assuming that it seems appropriate they take action, or if the consequences appear to be too risky they move to a second option. All of this is done in an instant.

The key ingredient that enables these crisis workers to make quality split second decisions appears to be the extent of their experience. This suggests that intuition is not something mystical that only a few people possess, but rather something that we all possess and with training and experience can develop over time. As Saul explains, "The offensive force is the swirling uncertainty of our imagination. Intuition is our reaction to the movement."[38] It is the basis of action that does not have the luxury of slow consideration. Robinson[39] offers the following suggestions as to when intuition is most helpful to leaders:

- When there is insufficient data or not enough time to gather data.
- When there is too much information, or the data are conflicting.
- When data seem to support several options.
- When decisions have to be made on the spur of the moment, without time for data gathering.
- When a group's vision has grown cloudy and/or its mission seems inappropriate or obsolete.
- When there is a need to determine a new and inspiring vision and the overall direction for a group or organisation.
- When it is necessary to ensure that the abilities of all the individuals in the group or organisation are recognised and employed efficiently and effectively.

Intuition unbalanced by the other qualities, however, has the potential to lead to superstition, bigotry, and crisis management as leaders try to turn uncertainty into certainty. "Uncertainty is taken for normal, and the ability to embrace it as a sign of human consciousness as intelligence not fear."[40]

This raises the question of when does intuition seem to be a valid quality to employ and when does it become merely superstition or crisis management? The following examples provide some guidance:

- Intuition helps leaders size up a situation and unconsciously ask, what is happening here?
- Leaders use intuition to get a sense of trends. In the school closure process I described, I was constantly on the watch for trends within the committee. Was I pushing them too hard? Were factions beginning to coalesce? Were personal agendas overtaking the group processes?
- Successful leaders are readers of their resources. "Successful individuals think in terms of what *they*[41] can do. Successful leaders, on the other hand, see every situation in terms of resources: money, raw materials, technology and most important, people."[42]

- Intuitive leaders can sense what is happening amongst people and respond accordingly. My school closure committee was composed of ten people that I had never met. I had learned from my mentors not just to keep my mouth shut but to listen and read not only *what* was said but *how* it was said. My wife has the uncanny ability to read other people's emotions and attitudes in any situation by observing facial or body cues and watching the patterns of their behaviour. There have been many times that I have wished that I had her skill.

- Intuitive leaders have a sense of themselves: they understand their own strengths, weaknesses, and current state of mind in a situation.

- Intuitive leaders have a sense of timing. Intuitive leaders ask themselves the following questions:

   Do I have the political support from key stakeholders to pursue this course of action?

   Are the necessary resources available to continue to push forward?

   Are my key supporters sufficiently physically and mentally energised to continue?

   Are there other issues that must be attended to before we can continue?

   Do I have the energy to stay the course?

   Does our course of action still contribute to our organisational goals?

School and district leaders need to know when to move aggressively on an issue, to back off, speak up, shut up, or just cut their losses. The ability to read the context, the people involved and the resources available all come into this equation. In the case of the school closure committee, moving forward prematurely with recommendations would have resulted in conflict and community upset, but to let the process drag on indefinitely would have undermined the essential purpose of the committee. There were people on that committee who would have happily stalled until everyone just got tired and the whole project disbanded or dissolved. In the case of the cafeteria, timing was everything. It was important to have key allies in the business department and move at a time when district criticism of the outside contractor was widespread.

For leaders who have generally enjoyed success and made good intuitive decisions, it is easy to get seduced into making inappropriate intuitive judgements when more deliberative thought is required. I have described some of my more successful endeavours previously, but I have also made some very poor calls, especially personnel decisions where I allowed my heart to rule my head, when I operated on a purely intuitive level without calling on my other qualities of reason, ethics, imagination, and memory. As I became more experienced in my various roles I found the quality of my intuitive decisions improved, which anecdotally supports Klein's view that intuition is the way we translate our experiences into action.

Memory

The final quality of memory gives us the ability to shape our thinking and our actions in a balanced way. From it we grasp our context, our thoughts, our questions, our actions, our lives. It is the platform from which we initiate thought – without memory there is a vacuum – and propaganda thrives in a vacuum, as does ideology. "Functioning individuals and functioning societies require the context of memory in order to shape their thinking and their actions," but memory to the extreme, however, freezes our thoughts and actions in the past and distorts our other qualities and, as Saul further explains, "A rigid memory pretends to guarantee the future by freezing that of the past."[43] As a result habit can become "a labour saving device"[44] and a significant obstacle to change and improvement.

"Memory is part of a seamless web with the future, there to help us remember exactly what our civilization is constructed upon, and therefore, in what ways our civilization is shaped, in order to serve our needs and our interests."[45] In some ways memory is the enemy of the technocrat, who tends to operate as though each new day is another day and unconnected to yesterday. How else can we explain society's inability to learn from its mistakes? An understanding of how a school came to be the way it is provides an important contextual basis for understanding the directions it might need to take and some of the impediments in its way. Experience is important. Just because a person is experienced or older does not necessarily mean he or she suffers from 'hardening of the categories'. Leadership develops in large measure from experience – often learning from making mistakes.

I was fortunate as a young principal because the principal of the neighbouring school, who was nearing the end of a long and distinguished career, befriended me and became my mentor. There wasn't a situation that faced me that Mike Furlong hadn't already dealt with. I well remember the telephone call from a parent who told me that he and I were being sued for $100,000 (about £40,000). Apparently his son had tossed a candy (a sweet) to a girl in the school hitting her in the eye and her guardian had initiated a suit against anyone and everyone including the boy's father and me. Since the incident had not been reported, I knew nothing about it. After shaking myself out of my initial panic, I phoned Mike at home and told him my tale of woe. He laughed and said, "Hell, Dean, I've been sued at least three times, here is what you do." I followed Mike's guidance and sure enough the suit never amounted to anything. He was terrific in giving me advice on procedural and legal issues, and he in turn used me to work with his people in my areas of expertise. He also taught me the importance of humour in deflating tense situations and appearing calm even when things weren't calm on the inside. Although he passed away a number of years ago, I remember him fondly and remain grateful to him for guiding me through those early years. Memory is an important quality to develop or access. "Perhaps the greatest danger caused by years of downsizing and reengineering has been the tragic loss of wisdom from within organizations. In restructuring we have fired our elders and they were the keepers of our organizational wisdom."[46]

Conclusion

This chapter has suggested that the goal of leadership development is to help existing and potential educational leaders achieve a condition of 'flow' in which a person's skills are completely engaged in overcoming a particular challenge that is just about manageable. I have borrowed John Ralston Saul's idea that each of us possesses a 'tool kit' made up of the qualities of reason, ethics, common sense, imagination, intuition, and memory that we can develop and employ to meet the challenges of leadership that are ahead. Like a carpenter's tool kit, the tools must be used appropriately and compatibly so that they can produce impressive results. To the carpenter who only uses a hammer from the tool kit, everything becomes a nail and destruction follows. For leaders, the qualities in our 'tool kits' used separately or in an unbalanced way can easily produce irrationality, intolerance, superstition, fantasy, or just plain nonsense.

The challenge for those who design leadership programs, therefore, is to engage the 'qualities' of their existing and potential leaders. Leaders need to contemplate the history of reform in their country, share the many good practices that are available, and address such ethical issues as coaching only those students who will alter a school's placement on the results of standardised tests. They will need to engage their imaginations in envisioning possible alternative structures to enhance learning in schools, and to experience simulations that at once engage a person's intuition and common sense. Leadership development programs must infuse opportunities to engage and develop all of these qualities 'in equilibrium' throughout all their activities, rather than perpetuating the present practice of focusing on instrumental rationality and memory to the virtual exclusion of other qualities. If as suggested here, these six qualities are the vehicle through which we can engage potential leaders in their learning, then what do leaders of learning actually need to learn? The next chapter will attempt to answer this question.

Notes

1 Csikszentmihalyi, M. (2004). *Good Business: Leadership, flow, and the making of meaning*. New York: Penguin Books.
2 Collins and Porras (1994) op. cit., p. 217.
3 Csikszentmihalyi, op. cit., p. 31.
4 Ibid, p. 29.
5 Saul, J.R. (2001). *On Equilibrium*. Toronto: Penguin/Viking, p. 3.
6 Ibid, p. 5.
7 Ibid, p. 13.
8 Ibid, p. 16.
9 Saul, J.R. (1993). *Voltaire's Bastards: The dictatorship of reason in the West*. Toronto, ON: Penguin Books: Canada.
10 Giuliani, R. (2002) p. 154.
11 Collins and Porras (1994) op. cit., p. 215.

12 Author's emphasis.

13 Saul (2001) p. 272.

14 Ibid, p. 68.

15 Smith, A. (1984). *The Theory of Moral Sentiments.* Indianapolis, IN: Liberty Fund, p. 235.

16 Starratt, R. (1991). 'Building an ethical school: A theory of practice in educational leadership', *Educational Administration Quarterly*, 27 (2): pp. 185–202.

17 Begley, P.T. and Johansson, O. (eds) (2003). *The Ethical Dimensions of School Leadership.* Dordrecht, Netherlands: Kluwer Press.

18 Kidder, R.M. (1995). *How People Make Tough Choices.* New York: Morrow.

19 Saul (2001) op. cit., p. 86.

20 Ibid, p. 23.

21 Scaruffi, P. (2001). *Thinking about Thoughts: Consciousness, life and meaning*, at www. thymos.com/tat/common.html

22 Ibid, p. 23.

23 Tyack, D. and Tobin, W. (1994). 'The Grammar of Schooling: Why has it been so hard to change?', *American Educational Research Journal*, 31 (3): pp. 453–79.

24 Dolhenty, J. (2003). 'Philosophy and common sense', *Philosophy Resource Centre*, http://radicalacademy.com/studentrefphil.htm

25 This is the equivalent of a local inspector in the UK or assistant superintendent in the USA and some provinces of Canada.

26 In Ontario, elementary schools educate students from junior kindergarten to grade 8. Students begin school at four years of age and most attend secondary school in their fourteenth year. Secondary schools enrol students for four additional years.

27 Quoted in Peter, T. (2003). *Re-imagine!: Business excellence in a disruptive age.* New York: DK Publishing, p. 163.

28 Saul (2001) op. cit., p. 116.

29 Ibid, p. 118.

30 Ibid, p. 126.

31 Author's emphasis.

32 Hamel, G. (2003) op. cit., p. 411.

33 For a more in depth examination of this paradox see Fink, D. (2001). 'Two Solitudes: Policy makers and policy implementers', in M. Fielding (ed.), *Taking Education Really Seriously: Three years of hard labour.* London: Routledge/Falmer.

34 Boden, M. (1990). *The Creative Mind: Myths and mechanisms.* New York: Basic Books, p. 255.

35 Giuliani, R. (2002) op. cit., p. 55.

36 Saul (2001) op. cit., p. 170.

37 Klein, G. (2003). *Intuition at Work: Why developing your gut instincts makes you better at what you do.* New York: Doubleday.

38   Saul (2001) op. cit., p. 163.
39   Robinson, A. (1997). 'Intuition: A critical leadership skill', *Innovative Leader*, 6 (7): pp. 251–300.
40   Saul (2001) op. cit, p. 211.
41 My emphasis.
42 Maxwell, J.C. (1998). *The 21 Irrefutable Laws of Leadership*. Nashville, TN: Nelson.
43 Saul (2001) op. cit., p. 219.
44 Tyack and Tobin (1994) op. cit., p. 453.
45 Saul, J.R. (1993). *Voltaire's Bastards: The dictatorship of reason in the West*. Harmondsworth: Penguin, p. 136.
46 Secretan, L. (1996). *Reclaiming the Higher Ground: Creating organizations that inspire the soul*. Toronto, ON: Macmillan, p. 14.

5   *Learnings*

While I have already stated that we seem to be making educational leadership into something beyond the capabilities of reasonably talented mortals, and that 'designer leadership'[1]appears to be unattractive to potential leaders, the importance of leadership in an organisation remains one of the few ideas in the change literature about which there is consistent agreement.[2] The major educational reform movements all identify leadership as an important ingredient for educational change. Gronn[3] declares that "whatever the cultural, ethnic, gender and social class component of the context concerned, the two attributes which best define a leader are influence and identification, while 'leading' is defined as the framing of meaning and the mobilization of support for a meaningful course of action." This deceptively simple definition raises fundamental questions such as:

- How do leaders influence followers to pursue a course of action?

- Why do followers identify with leaders?

- How do leaders 'frame' meaning and mobilise followers?

- How do leaders define a 'meaningful' course of action?

The leadership literature until the 1980s tended to see leadership and leaders as 'doing things right'[4] – being efficient and managerial. This generation of "theories and studies was driven by assumptions about scientific management, rational decision making, positivist epistemology, and behavioristic psychology."[5] Burns[6] defined this style of leadership as transactional. Leithwood[7] explained that transactional leadership in education is "based on an exchange of services (from a teacher, for example) for various kinds of rewards (salary, recognition, intrinsic rewards) that the leader controls." Transactional leadership practices, some would claim, help people recognise what needs to be done in order to reach a desired outcome and may also increase their confidence and motivation. Sergiovanni[8] described this view of leadership as "what is rewarded gets done."

Leithwood and his colleagues[9] have outlined seven major approaches to leadership that currently influence educational policy and practice – managerial, contingent, instructional, transactional, moral, transformational, and participative. The first five models tend to be more 'instrumental' in design.[10] In each model, formal leaders attempt to influence followers to achieve organisational goals by employing various sources of power – the positional power of the manager or contingent leader, the expertise of the instructional leader,[11] or the system values of the moral leader.[12] These goals or 'meaningful courses of action' include ensuring the efficient completion of specified tasks (managerial), responding effectively to organisational challenges (contingent), enhancing the effectiveness of teachers' classroom practice (instructional) and increasing the effectiveness of decisions and staff involvement in these decisions (moral). In spite of many alternative models of leadership these more technocratic approaches still tend to dominate policy and practice.[13]

The other two styles described by Leithwood and his colleagues,[14] transformational and participative leadership, require formal leaders to involve the larger group in decision-making activities to ensure organisational improvement. These models are derived from Burns's[15] concept of transformational leadership and subsume such approaches as 'visionary' leadership[16] and 'charismatic' leadership.[17] These more inclusive avenues to leadership focus on effectiveness or "doing right things."[18] Leithwood and his colleagues[19] argue that transformational leadership moves schools beyond first order or surface changes to second order changes that alter the 'core technologies' of schooling. This leadership style includes the pursuit of common goals, empowerment and the maintenance of a collaborative culture, teacher development and problem solving.[20] These qualities are reflected in teacher-led professional development committees, mentorship programs, teacher-initiated curriculum innovation, and staff-led school planning teams. Both collaborative styles – transformational and participative – are intended to involve people in organisations in the decisions that will increase an organisation's capacity to improve and respond to changes in its context.

The implication in most of this work is that leaders should 'transform' their organisations through substantive models of leadership that focus on the meaning, mission and identity of the organisation as a whole. As I reflect on my own career, however, I find these categories artificial and disconnected from my reality. I was both a manager and a leader, transactional and transformational, contingent and participative. On occasions such as with the teacher who habitually swore at children, I was quite authoritarian, and in issues that involved the entire staff, such as developing a school-wide development plan, I was required to be quite democratic. Deal and Peterson[21] amongst others have criticised the 'artificial debate' between management and leadership and have suggested that schools require leadership that blends both the technical skills of the engineer and the creative imagination of the artist. They declare that:

> High performing organisations have both order and meaning, structure and values. They achieve quality at reasonable costs. They accomplish goals while attending to core values and beliefs. They encourage both fundamentals and fun. They embrace the dialectic between expression of values and accomplishment of goals. They encourage both leadership and management, symbolic behavior and technical activity.[22]

The educational administration literature generally supports this view.[23] One only need look at the diversity of roles played by educational leaders to recognise that most adopt many styles of leadership depending on the situation. Some critics have even argued that transformational leadership and similar participative approaches are, in practice, 'instrumental' in nature and just less overt 'techniques' or strategies to colonise teachers into co-operating with top-down changes in which they find little meaning.[24] Gronn contends that transformational leadership "reduces leadership to something that goes on in the head of the leader: devoid of any recognition of follower attribution and implicit theories, nor is it aware that leadership is a socially constructed process."[25] It would appear that, at least in a school context, both transactional and transformational models of leadership have serious conceptual and practical flaws.

A third body of work on leadership is emerging that is influenced by complexity theory[26] and the literature on school reculturing.[27]

Stacey,[28] for example, suggests that instrumental views of leadership that are based on a rational, predictable, linear world are limited in times of diversity, complexity, and unpredictability, and that more democratic and inclusive models of leadership are required. Riley captures this idea in her description of 'distributive leadership'. "It sees leadership as a network of relationships among people, structures and cultures (both within and across organizational boundaries), not just as a role based function assigned to, or acquired by, a person in an organization, who then uses his or her power to influence the actions of others ... Leadership is seen as an organic activity, dependent on interrelationships and connections."[29] Spillane and his colleagues'[30] concept of 'distributed' leadership develops similar ideas. The notion of distributed or distributive leadership fundamentally changes the role of formal leaders. As Block[31] suggests, leaders in the future will be required to exercise stewardship rather than leadership; he defines stewardship as the willingness to be accountable for the well being of the larger organisation by operating in service rather than in control.

In summary, the literature on leadership styles describes two general approaches to the ways leaders influence others to achieve organisational goals – one set of strategies can be described as 'instrumental', and the second as 'empowering'. Instrumental strategies can be overt, such as a demand for compliance, or subtle, such as involving teachers in committees in which the goals are predetermined. Regardless of the style, instrumental strategies represent the calculated and sometimes cynical ways employed in order to 'influence' others to improve their procedures and practices, and to submit to sources of power that reside outside themselves and their school community. Conversely, leaders who empower others distribute leadership widely throughout the school community, and empower colleagues "to evaluate what goals are important and what conditions are helpful."[32] 'Instrumental' leaders lead from the apex of the pyramid whereas 'empowering' leaders operate from the centre of a web of human relationships.[33] While the scholarly evidence encourages leaders to influence through empowering strategies, both they and school principals in particular often confront a reality in most western jurisdictions of multiple, intrusive and often conflicting policy pressures that demand urgent and demonstrable evidence of improved student outcomes.[34] Traditional Public

Administration and New Public Management, described in Chapter 1, have obliged leaders to adopt overt or more cunning instrumental strategies to achieve results. It is this paradox between the rhetoric of empowerment and the pressure to impose mandated changes on reluctant teachers that bedevils school leaders and has accelerated the early retirement of many quality leaders.

In learning communities, however, leaders empower their colleagues to work collaboratively to achieve organisational goals in which they collectively find meaning. For principals and other school and district leaders, Dufour captures this idea when he states, "When learning becomes the preoccupation of the school, when all the school's educators examine the efforts and initiatives of the school through the lens of their impact on learning, the structure and culture of the school begin to change in substantive ways. School leaders contribute when they shift their emphasis from helping individual teachers improve their instruction to helping teams of teachers ensure that students achieve intended outcomes of their schooling."[35]

'Learnings' for leaders of learning

To prepare leaders for a future as leaders of learning as described by Dufour, we need to identify, recruit, prepare, select, and support leaders around a set of 'leaders' learnings' that are not bounded by time and space or collected in huge lists of 'best' practices. These learnings are sufficiently flexible to apply regardless of the context or career stage of a leader. To describe these essential learnings in terms of practice the following section follows the journey of Charmaine Watson as she sets out to turn Wayvern School into a student-learning centred school.

After four years as principal at Talisman Park High School, district officials transferred Watson to Wayvern School to address a potential crisis situation. She replaced a retiring principal who had spent four years at Wayvern and seemed incapable of responding to the significant social and political issues that affected the school. Upset by her inability to complete the job at Talisman Park, Charmaine recognised that her district was in a tight spot and reluctantly agreed to address Wayvern's dilemma. After four years as assistant principal and four years as principal, the district leadership felt that she was the person to address the challenging contextual situation at her new school. Her first task at Wayvern then was to find out "what is happening here?"

Contextual knowledge

Successful leaders make connections by developing firm knowledge and understanding of their contexts. Context relates to the particular situation, background, or environment in which something is happening. Internal context includes the students, subjects and departments, and the school itself; external context encompasses, among other influences, the district or local education authority of which the school is a part, the school's parent and neighbouring community, the relevant employee unions, and the appropriate government(s) of the day. The research evidence is fairly clear – schools can only be understood in their context.[36] The following account is the result of lengthy interviews with Charmaine Watson and research based on the Changing Frames project.[37]

Charmaine inherited a school that had a reputation during the 1970s as a progressive 'lighthouse school'. It was the only school in the region that combined grade 7 through to secondary school completion. Teachers in the 1970s and 1980s taught at all levels and worked to create coherent, quality programs for both the elementary component of the school (grades 7 and 8 – 12 and 13 year old students) and the secondary (grades 9 to 12 – 14 to 18 year old students). Over the years, however, the 'light in the lighthouse' had gradually burned out and the school had experienced what I have called elsewhere an 'attrition of change'.[38] Leaders departed to other schools; some teachers got older and more set in their ways and less engaged in the life of the school; new teachers joined the staff with little understanding of its initiating vision and values, and the established staff did very little to induct them into the school's culture. Perhaps the most debilitating factor that contributed to the 'attrition of change' was the entrenched attitude of the unions. The unions that represented elementary and secondary teachers haggled over staffing patterns. This created two schools within one building and undermined the rationale for the school, relegating the elementary teachers to second-class citizenship, because provincial funding formulas and school policies meant that they had a greater workload and fewer teaching resources than their secondary colleagues. In addition, the district assigned an assistant principal with elementary (primary) qualifications to report to the principal on behalf of the elementary section of the school. Unfortunately for the continuity of planning and representation in the elementary section, the district used Wayvern as a training-ground for potential elementary principals, and moved the elementary assistant principal almost annually. Enrolment in grades 7 and 8 dropped precipitously because middle-class parents preferred the more upscale kindergarten of the grade 8 school nearby. Charmaine's predecessor exacerbated the problem by actively favouring the secondary component and paying little attention to the elementary sector of the school. By the time Charmaine arrived on the scene, this divide was a chasm.

In 1998 when Charmaine became its principal, Wayvern enrolled 1,300 secondary students, and 250 elementary students. One hundred and fifty eight students from both panels (phases) were English as Second Language (ESL) students. Moreover, the school's demographics had shifted from its middle-class origins to a multi-cultural multi-racial community as successive waves of immigrants moved into the region throughout the 1980s and 1990s. Boundary changes that added the children of mostly working-class parents housed in high-rise buildings and government subsidised housing also contributed to an altered social structure. To make the situation even more challenging, Charmaine had to take over a school in which the government's cost-cutting had resulted in the loss of 17 teachers and a staff that was both grieving for departed colleagues, and angry that they had had to pick up their workload. Moreover, she had to address parental concerns about the safety of their children in the school, declining student enrolment, chronic social issues created by the school's changing demographics and some serious questioning of the efficacy of the student learning program by some parents and teachers.

As an experienced and observant leader, Charmaine had learned strategies to analyse Wayvern's internal and external contexts and to respond to their unique characteristics. She scrutinised student results, examined attendance and discipline data, assessed the qualifications and capacity of her staff, and over the course of the first six months developed an entry plan designed to answer her question 'what's going on here?' This plan involved interviewing every staff member, many students, and a number of parents. As well as reviewing the information yielded by observable data, context-aware leaders like Charmaine find out how the students, parents, and staff feel about the school as a way to discover the deeper social context in which their school resides. Her interviews and meetings revealed a major source of the morale problems resided in micro-political issues within the school, and macro-political issues involving her Parents' Council[39] and influential parents.

Political acumen

Political acumen is a key 'learning' for leaders and Charmaine could draw on her experience and training to address political issues both inside and outside of the school. At a micro-level, schools are filled with groups and individuals with different interests, and varying degrees of power that occasionally lead to conflict. Leaders use political methods, such as negotiation and coalition building, to move schools toward mutually agreed goals. In addition to the elementary-secondary split, Charmaine identified four significant micro-political factions – the guardians of the vision who had taught in the school for over twenty-five years and nostalgically pined for the old days as the 'lighthouse school'; an 'old guard' who resented the previous principal, hated the government, who had become cynical and disillusioned and were counting the days until retirement; a cadre of younger teachers who loved the school and were keen to get involved in meaningful activities; and a group of very inexperienced teachers who were just trying to survive. Certain departments, such as mathematics, science and English, held greater sway than more marginalised areas such as the arts and technical and vocational subjects.

Charmaine's entry process revealed a great deal, but her intuition had to 'fill in the blanks'. As she stated, "Your skin tells you what's what." She sensed that the previous principal had created a 'low trust' environment, so in her early days in the school she used every possible way to communicate her concern for students, and her willingness to be open, forthcoming, and fair. One of her first tasks was to replace her head of counselling who had moved to another school. It was widely assumed that one of the 'old guard', the department assistant head, would inherit the job. Charmaine declared to the staff that anyone with qualifications was eligible and made the entire process quite transparent by writing an open letter to them delineating in detail how the process would unfold and who would be involved. Significantly, both the elementary and secondary assistant principals were on the selection committee. This sent a message to staff concerning the significance of the elementary sector. The staff applauded the choice of a woman directly from the teaching ranks. The decision had the effect of communicating another message that 'things are going to be different'. To further convey her commitment to the idea of students first, she terminated efforts to upgrade the administrative offices to free up money for student programs. Both acts were symbolic and important. She delegated significant leadership opportunities to department heads and school committees, ensuring that they had clear goals, regular feedback, and the training and support they needed to do their jobs. Like Ronald Reagan she operated on the premise of 'trust but verify'. In addition, she ensured that all committees and other staff functions included broad representation from every department, particularly the marginalised ones. To shift the status of the elementary component of the school, she treated it as a department and included it in all activities, committees and decisions. By using her micro-political skills such as negotiation, coalition building, and ensuring representative structures, she gradually built the staff into a more cohesive, goals-driven group.

School leaders also must represent the interests of their schools with their governing bodies, communities, and government agencies. Politics is about power and influence and to ignore political issues or consider that political activity is unworthy of a leader is to leave the school, its staff, students and parents, vulnerable to competing social forces. Charmaine faced a burning issue with parents over the safety of students that the previous principal had neglected. As an acknowledged expert in the topic, which was one of the reasons the district leaders assigned her to the school, she determined to work closely with the school's Parents' Council as a problem-solving group. Her predecessor had treated this group as more of a nuisance so Charmaine engaged it directly to address the safety problems. Rather than them just complaining, she challenged the Council to be part of the solution. By once again being open and transparent and also expecting performance on behalf of the students, she gradually got the parents on her side and together they attended to the legitimate safety concerns. She also made a particular point of engaging with the parents of elementary students. Since her predecessor had delegated this to the transient elementary assistant principals, she showed up at every elementary school event as well as the secondary school functions. During her tenure, the flow of students to the neighbouring school reversed, and Wayvern's enrolments increased significantly, particularly at the elementary level. In spite of her own exhaustion, Charmaine's pervasive visibility reinforced her commitment to student learning and her values of openness, fairness, and engagement.

Emotional understanding

To create an environment in which teachers find 'flow'[40] requires leaders with emotional understanding. Such leaders learn to read the emotional responses of those around them and create emotional bonds with and among those with whom they interact. Charmaine knew that her arrival would meet with apprehension and distrust on the part of some, and enthusiasm from those others who disliked her predecessor. Unlike her predecessor she played no favourites. Her message to everyone was the same – transparency, fairness, and a focus on student learning. Moreover, she walked her talk by ensuring that hiring processes, decision making, and goal setting, engaged appropriate staff members and were transparent to all.

Most importantly, Charmaine established emotional connections with some of the more entrenched staff by acknowledging the school's innovative past, and particularly the family feeling that the school once possessed. Andy Hargreaves[41] explains that the emotions of educational change most commonly addressed are those which help to defuse so-called 'resistance' to change, like trust, support, involvement, commitment to teamwork, and willingness to experiment. Through committee structures, leadership reorganisation and distributing leadership, Charmaine gradually reduced resistance to a very few teachers who over her four year tenure at the school gradually found themselves becoming more isolated. At the same time she took decisive action to deal with under-performing staff members. In her first few years she dismissed a particularly difficult teachers' assistant, demoted an ineffective department head, and at the time of my interviews with her was dealing with two teachers on performance issues. Ironically, her decisive actions only improved her stature with staff. They saw for the first time in many years a leader who dealt decisively with poor performance and unprofessional behaviour.

Hargreaves also contends that leaders with emotional understanding lead colleagues into uncharted territory on a change journey through impassioned and critical engagement or the critique of ideas, purposes, and practices. For Charmaine, the imminent provincial literacy test for all grade 10 students provided a useful vehicle to engage in an intellectual and professional journey. As she stated to her staff "Let's keep doing what we know we are doing well. Let's look at this as an opportunity. How are we going to make the best of this (literacy test) in our own way?" This was the genesis of the school-wide literacy approach. By turning a literacy test that other schools considered a threat and a problem limited to a few English teachers into a school-wide movement, Charmaine emotionally engaged the staff in a cause to which they could almost all subscribe. Similarly, she reached out to her parent community that had felt ignored and undervalued. By engaging her Parents' Council in problem-solving activities and attending events that her predecessor had avoided, she developed a relationship with the community that produced a favourable climate for the school and which showed itself in the school's increased enrolment.

Understanding learning

As I have outlined in some depth in Chapter 2, leaders need to have a deep, current, and critical understanding of the learning process to promote learning and support others' learning. Not only do they need to have insight into 'deep' learning for students, they must also have a 'deep' understanding of how adults learn if they are to support teachers' learning and thus must be able to mobilise the school's human and material resources for this purpose. Charmaine made student learning her chief priority and engaged the entire staff in the literacy initiative that spanned out into a related investigation into alternative strategies for student assessment. As a former English department head herself, she was able to connect her staff's literacy committee with the 'Language across the Curriculum' work that was widespread in Ontario in the 1980s, and to direct their energies into productive avenues. When the government forced school boards to reduce their payrolls, the schools were obliged to cut the number of department heads and to eliminate all assistant department head positions. Charmaine, however, treated this threat to staff harmony as an opportunity. Unlike other schools that had created separate headships to address literacy and assessment thereby compartmentalising them into 'fiefdoms', she altered the job expectations for heads to ensure that all subject department heads had a commitment to these topics.

By once again being totally transparent about the selection process and focusing on what was best for student learning, Charmaine turned a potentially destructive situation into a positive process. In addition, she lobbied her superiors in the system to ensure that her assistant principals, both of whom had strong curriculum backgrounds, remained in the school. She was successful in ending the almost annual rotation of the assistant principal responsible for grades 7 and 8. With the structure in place, and the senior managers working as an effective team, Charmaine and her assistants harnessed her staff's learning in support of student learning. Her school's immediate results on the literacy test were not spectacular, but within two years Wayvern had finished second in the district, ahead of most of the middle-class schools in the up-scale neighbourhoods.

Critical thinking

What tends to differentiate effective and ineffective leaders is the quality of their judgements: whether their decisions work for the students in the long term. Knowing and remembering to ask the right questions depends on both wisdom and judgement.[42] A significant part of a formal leader's job is to act as a gatekeeper, to ask the right questions, to know what initiatives to support, what to oppose, and what to subvert. This question-asking facility is a necessary 'learning' to enable leaders to help to develop a school's capacity to deal with change. Charmaine Watson was an expert problem seeker as well as problem solver. Her entry process consisted of an on-going, pervasive search for an understanding of the school, its history, demographics and culture. One of her earliest acts was to engage interested staff in the Changing Frames project described in Chapter 3 to help them to understand the dynamics of change and to become better problem seekers. The way her staff responded to the literacy test through a school-wide initiative on 'deep' literacy learning demonstrated that they had become expert problem seekers and problem solvers.

Making connections

It is also a leader's role to view the entire organisation as a whole and help stakeholders to view the school in an holistic way. Leaders provide coherence and make connections so others can see the interrelationships and interconnections of the many things happening in a school. The development of a school-wide perspective is an important 'learning' to promote positive change. By the time Charmaine retired from education to pursue further studies Wayvern had evolved – from a school that was balkanised into departmental islands, fractured by a split between its elementary and secondary components, and estranged from its community – into a cohesive, collaborative unit. She achieved this result by making some strategic staffing moves, energising the staff's latent desire to recreate its dynamic past, mobilising support from the district and the school's Parents' Council and community, and by consistently advocating and modelling her values of openness, fairness and dedication to 'deep' student learning.

Futures thinking

Successful leaders must learn how to connect the past, the present, and the future. Leaders' awareness and understanding of forces influencing the life of a school are crucial to shaping a school community's shared sense of vision in productive and inspiring ways.

Leaders should also be aware of shifting currents in local political, social and economic forces and should help staff to understand the connections between and among global, national and local forces. Anticipating the future enables leaders to help colleagues act strategically rather than randomly as they journey into the future.[43]

Elsewhere, Andy Hargreaves and I have described the following seven principles of sustainable leadership:[44]

- Leadership that sustains learning for all students and that nourishes their development.

- Leadership that lasts, that endures over time, that stretches across individuals and that leaves a lasting legacy of deep and enduring learning for students.

- Leadership that does not damage the surrounding environment, that does not drain the leadership resources of other schools to support initiatives in one or two lighthouse or showplace schools.

- Leadership that can be supported by available or achievable resources – human as well as financial.

- Leadership that is a shared responsibility; sustainable leadership involves everyone, and does not rest on the shoulders of the few.

- Leadership that is self-sustaining, sustaining selves that have the emotional resources and system supports to avoid burnout and maintain their impact over time.

- Leadership that promotes diversity and builds capacity throughout the educational environment – that fosters many versions of excellence, and the means of sharing them through powerful learning communities.[45]

If one reviews Charmaine's tenure at Wayvern, she purposely and intuitively addressed all seven of these principles. She and her staff concentrated on aspects of the school that mattered, like deep learning in literacy. To this end they created structures and developed a school culture that continues in the directions she initiated, and as a result the school's students still achieve well above what could be expected when one considers the school's demographics. Wayvern's achievement was accomplished without special resources, but rather by the school employing existing resources carefully and purpose-fully to support school goals. The school's success was not at the expense of schools in the surrounding area as so often occurs in change efforts. What Charmaine did particularly well, however, was to share leadership widely. Not only did she distribute real school-wide leadership opportunities to formal leaders like her assistants and department heads, but she also engaged the staff through action committees to address crucial school issues like literacy and assess-ment for learning. By maintaining a positive, optimistic outlook, supported by purposeful activity she successfully turned the per-ceived threats posed by a seemingly uncaring Ontario government into opportunities to improve the school and address student learn-ing in purposeful ways.

There is no doubt that Wayvern's teachers felt as deeply antago-nised by the policies of the Ontario government as teachers in other schools, but rather than becoming apathetic or immobilised by anger as occurred elsewhere, Wayvern's teachers got on with their profes-sional duties. They attended to the vast array of learning needs of their multi-cultural, multi-racial students and developed a variety of teaching strategies to promote student literacy in all the subject areas, learning how to employ alternative assessment strategies as vehicles for enhanced student learning. By concentrating on these principles, Charmaine could depart feeling confident that what she had initiated would be sustained over time and that her empowering approach to leadership had worked to enhance student learning.

Conclusion

This chapter has suggested that descriptions of leadership have tended to fall into two broad categories; the instrumental style where some leaders use various sources of power to get teachers to commit to changes in which they find little meaning, and the alter-native style where leaders like Charmaine Watson use empowering strategies, engaging colleagues in determining the directions of the changes in which they are to be involved before setting out on the journey. Her leadership at Wayvern exemplified the model outlined in this book. She combined her dedication to student learning and her clearly articulated and modelled values, with her well-developed intellectual 'tool kit' and the essential 'learnings' of a leader of learning, to produce a student-learning centred school. By the time she left Wayvern, Charmaine had become a much more differentiated person, but also as a result of her experiences, a much more integrated individual. As stated in Chapter 4, a person who is more fully differentiated and integrated becomes the complex individual who "has the best chance at leading a happy, vital, and meaningful life."[46] Previous chapters have focused on the ways in which leaders differentiate themselves. The next chapter completes this equation by examining a leader's journey from outsider to trusted and integrated insider within a school's 'communities of practice'.

Notes

[1] Gronn, P. (1996). 'From transactions to transformations: A new world order in the study of leadership', *Educational Management & Administration,* 24 (1): pp. 7–30.

[2] Sammons, P., Mortimore, P. and Hillman, J. (1995). *Key Characteristics of Effective Schools: A review of school effectiveness research.* London: Office for Standards in Education; Fullan, M.G. (1993) *Change forces: Probing the depths of educational reform.* London: Falmer Press; Stoll, L., Fink, D. and Earl, L. (2002) *It's About Learning (and It's About Time).* London: Routledge/Falmer.

[3] Gronn, op. cit., p. 8.

[4] Bennis, W. and Nanus, B. (1985). *Leaders.* New York: Harper and Row.

[5] Leithwood, K. (1992). 'The move towards transformational leadership', *Educational Leadership,* 49: 5 pp. 8–12; p. 9.

[6] Burns, J.M. (1978). *Leadership.* New York: Harper and Row.

[7] Leithwood, ibid, p. 8.

[8] Sergiovanni, T. (1992*). Moral Leadership: Getting to the heart of school improvement.* San Francisco, CA: Jossey-Bass, p. 26.

[9] Leithwood, K.A., Jantzi, D. and Steinbach, R. (1999). *Changing Leadership for Changing Times.* Buckingham, UK: Open University Press.

[10] Sergiovanni, T. and Starratt, R. (1988). *Supervision: Human perspectives,* 4th edition. New York: McGraw-Hill.

[11] Smith, W.F. and Andrews, R.L. (1989). *Instructional Leadership: How principals make a difference.* Alexandria, VA: Association for Supervision and Curriculum Development.

[12] Sergiovanni, T. (1992a); Sergiovanni, T. (1992b). op. cit. San Francisco, CA: Jossey-Bass, p. 26.

[13] Saul, J.R. (1993). *Voltaire's Bastards: The dictatorship of reason in the*

West. Harmondsworth: Penguin.

14 Leithwood et al. (1999) op. cit., p. 23.

15 Burns (1978) op. cit.

16 Bass, B.M. (1985). *Leadership and Performance Beyond Expectations.* New York: The Free Press.

17 House, R.J. and Shamir, B. (1993). 'Towards the integration of trans-formational, charismatic, and visionary theories', in M.M. Chemers and R. Ayman (eds), *Leadership Theory and Research Perspectives and Directions.* San Diego, CA: Academic Press, pp. 81–107.

18 Bennis and Nanus (1985) op. cit.

19 Leithwood et al. (1999) op. cit.

20 Leithwood (1992) op. cit.

21 Deal, T.E. and Peterson, K. (1994). *The Leadership Paradox: Balancing logic and artistry in schools.* San Francisco, CA: Jossey-Bass.

22 Deal and Peterson (1994) op. cit., p. 9.

23 Louis, K.S-. and Miles, M.B. (1990). *Improving the Urban High School: What works and why.* New York: Teachers' College Press; Stoll and Fink (1996) op. cit.

24 Alix, N.M. (2000). 'Transformational leadership: Democratic or despotic?', *Educational Management & Administration,* 28 (1): pp. 7–20.

25 Gronn (1996) op. cit., p. 21.

26 Wheatley, M. (1994). *Leadership and the New Science.* San Francisco, CA: Berrett-Koehler; Morrison, K. (2002) *School Leadership and Complexity Theory.* London: Routledge/Falmer.

27 Hargreaves, A. (1994). *Changing Teachers, Changing Times: Teachers' work and culture in the postmodern age.* Toronto, ON: The Ontario Institute for Studies of Education of the University of Toronto; Wonycott-Kytle, A.M. and Bogotch, I.E. (1997) 'Reculturing: assumptions, beliefs, and values underlying the processes of restructuring', *Journal of School Leadership,* 7 (1): pp. 27–49.

28 Stacey, R. (1995). *Managing Chaos.* London: Kogan Page.

29 Riley, K. (2000). 'Leadership, learning and systemic change', *Journal of Educational Change,* 1 (1): pp. 57–75, p. 47.

30 Spillane, J.P., Halverson, R. and Drummond, J.B. (2001). 'Investigating school leadership practice: A distributed perspective', *Educational Researcher,* 30 (3): pp. 23–8.

31 Block, P. (1993). *Stewardship: Choosing service over self interest.* San Francisco, CA: Berrett-Koehler.

32 Foster, W. (1986). *Paradigms and Promises: New approaches to educational administration.* Buffalo, NY: Prometheus Books, pp. 185–6.

33 Murphy, J. (1994). 'Transformational change and the evolving role of the school principal', in J.Murphy and K. Seashore-Louis (eds), *Reshaping the Principalship: Insights from transforational reform efforts.* Thousand Oaks, CA: Corwin.

34 Hargreaves, A., Shaw, P., Fink, D., Retallick, J., Giles, C., Moore, S., Schmidt, M. and James-Watson, S. (2000). *Change Frames: Supporting secondary teachers in interpreting and integrating secondary school reform*. Toronto, ON: Ontario Institute for Studies in Education/University of Toronto; Fielding, M. (2001) (ed.), *Taking Education Really Seriously: Three years of hard labour*. London: Routledge/Falmer.

35 Dufour, R. (2002). 'The learning centred principal', *Educational Leadership*, 58 (8): p. 13.

36 Hallinger, P. and Murphy, J. (1986). 'The social context of effective schools', *American Journal of Education*, 94 (3): pp. 328–55; Teddlie, C. and Stringfield, S. (1993) *Schools Make a Difference: Lessons learned from a 10 year study of school effects*. New York: Teachers' College Press.

37 Hargreaves, A., Shaw, P., Fink, D., Retallick, J., Giles, C., Moore, S., Schmidt, M., and James-Watson, S. (2000). *Change Frames: Supporting secondary teachers in interpreting and integrating secondary school reform*. Toronto, ON: Ontario Institute for Studies in Education/University of Toronto.

38 Fink, D. (2000). *Good School, Real School: Why school reform doesn't last*. New York: Teachers' College Press, p. xiii.

39 In Ontario, each school must have an elected Parents' Council. These councils review budgets, school plans and personnel decisions. They provide an advisory function, but have no decision-making powers such as school governors in the UK, and New Zealand.

40 Csikszentmihalyi, M. (2004) op. cit.

41 Hargreaves, A. (1998). 'The emotional politics of teaching and teacher development: with implications for educational leadership', *International Journal for Leadership in Education*, 1 (4): pp. 316–36.

42 Secretan (1996) op. cit.

43 Davies, B. and Ellison, L. (1999). *Strategic Development and Direction of the School*. London: Routledge.

44 Hargreaves, A. and Fink, D. (2004). 'Seven principles of sustainable leadership', *Educational Leadership*, 61 (7): pp. 9–13. See also Hargreaves, A. and Fink, D. (2005) *Sustainable Leadership*. San Francisco, CA: Jossey-Bass.

45 See our book (Hargreaves, A. and Fink, D. [forthcoming] *Sustainable Leadership*. San Francisco, CA: Jossey-Bass), for an in depth discussion of these principles.

46 Csikszentmihalyi, M. (2004) op. cit., p. 29.

6 *Trajectories*

Have you ever looked closely at a spider's web? It is one of nature's wonders. A spider begins with one long thread and hopes that the wind will attach it to a stationary object to create a 'U'-shaped structure, and then it extends a thread downward from the 'U'-shaped structure and reinforces it with another to create a central configuration shaped like a 'Y'. Now the spider builds the outer perimeter extending from the points of the 'Y' and connects threads from the inner 'Y' structure to the perimeter. With this framework in place it slowly, but persistently, fills in the web with parallel almost concentric circles to complete the web. If you think about it, a web is a useful way to understand the complexity of organisations like schools and districts. Organisations have an essential skeletal structure of rules and regulations that determine relationships among people and tasks, distribute political power, and guide daily practice. It is this formal arrangement that appears in policy documents, organisational charts, written contracts, and budgets. It is the informal interconnections and interrelationships among the people that cut across these formal structures, however, or what Capra calls "the fluid and fluctuating networks of communications" that give the web its "aliveness."[1]

> The aliveness of an organization – its flexibility, creative potential and learning capability – resides in its informal 'communities of practice'. The formal parts of an organization may be 'alive' to varying degrees depending on how closely they are in touch with their informal networks.[2]

Everything and everyone in a web are connected in some way. When one touches a spider's web, the sensation reverberates from the point of contact throughout the entire web. Human organisations are similar. An action or situation in one part of the web affects all other parts of the web to a greater or lesser extent depending on one's location in the web. For example, one brilliant teacher in a classroom can set a positive tone throughout the school and community. Conversely, one particularly lethal teacher in a classroom can not only influence the children in that classroom, but can indirectly impact on all the children and teachers in all the classrooms in the school, as well as affect the community's attitudes towards the school. To carry this metaphor of 'school as web' one step further, consider every intersection where threads of common interest and association intersect in the web as a 'community of practice'.

Communities of practice

Communities of practice are everywhere in our daily lives and particularly in the organisations in which we work; they exist within our families, service organisations, recreational activities, and our churches. They are present wherever people voluntarily come together for mutual engagement and develop over time a shared repertoire of how they do things together. Communities of practice are not necessarily synonymous with a department or a team or other similar organisational units, although such formal structures can evolve into 'communities of practice'. Wenger[3] explains that,

> developing a practice requires the formation of a community whose members can engage with one another and thus acknowledge each other as participants. As a consequence, practice entails the negotiation of ways of being a person in that context ... the formation of a community of practice is also the negotiation of identities.[4]

He suggests that "our identities form in a ... kind of tension between our investment in various forms of belonging and our ability to negotiate the meanings that matter in those contexts."[5] Identity formation is the result of the interplay between one's *identification* with a community of practice and one's ability to *negotiate* meaning within that community. Identity is a "constant becoming" and we "constantly renegotiate through the course of our lives."[6] He explains that when we have negotiated an identity within a community of practice in which we are a full member,

> we are in familiar territory. We can handle ourselves competently. We experience competence and are recognized as competent. We know how to engage with others. We understand why they do what they do because we understand the enterprise to which participants are accountable. Moreover, we share the resources they use to communicate and go about their activities. These dimensions of competence ... become dimensions of identity.[7]

Schools have many 'communities of practice'. There are the teachers of grade 4 (Key Stage 2) who voluntarily work together on the children's learning program, or the teachers of physical education who agree to ensure that all children are involved in daily physical fitness activities, or the football coaches who come together to institute a similar system of play for all the school teams. A 'community of practice' might include the group who meet annually to prepare for the school's graduation ceremonies, or the union representatives who work together to present a common front on workload issues to the principal, or the teachers' assistants who develop a supportive relationship to enhance their collective profile in the school. Other 'communities' might involve the teachers of music and visual and performing arts who decide to organise a school-wide arts festival, or groups which come together to support each other in the face of bewildering changes.

Some of these communities contribute significantly to student learning and others may actually get in the way. The list could go on and depends totally on context and the nature of a school's leadership. There are no membership cards in these communities, some don't even have names, but everyone who is a member of a community of practice knows who its members are. Some individuals will belong to a number of communities and easily traverse various community boundaries. For leaders moving into a school with a multiplicity of communities the challenges are formidable. Firstly, the leader has to learn what communities exist, and how they function. Secondly, the leader has to determine if these communities are contributing to student learning or impeding school goals. Finally, the leader must find ways to influence and focus the various communities within this complex web of relationships to create a genuine school-wide learning community that supports student learning. These webs are not structureless, but structured according to a different logic from the traditional factory metaphor with its assembly line, bureaucracy and hierarchies that shape most educational organisations.

In a web, as Henry Mintzberg[8] explains,

> Management has to be *everywhere*. It has to flow with the activity, which itself can not be predicted or *formalized* ... Management also has to be potentially everyone. In a network, responsibility for making decisions and developing strategic initiatives has to be distributed, so that responsibility can flow to whoever is best able to deal with the issue at hand.

In webs or networks, control has to give way to collaboration. They have no centre or apex, just a multiplicity of connections and threads that link various communities that leaders must try to understand and influence to achieve organisational goals. Mintzberg adds that "bosses and subordinates running up and down the hierarchy have to give way to the shifting back and forth between 'colleagues' on the inside and 'partners' on the outside." Webs need designated leaders to connect and contribute not command and control. "And that means that managers have to get inside those networks. Not be parachuted in, without knowledge, yet intent on leading the team. No, they must be deeply involved, to *earn* any leadership they can provide."[9] He contends that leadership within the organisational logic of a web is:

> not about taking clever decisions and making bigger deals, least of all for personal gains. It is about energizing other people to make better decisions and do better things ... it is about releasing the positive energy that exists naturally within people. Effective leadership inspires more than empowers; it connects more than it controls; it demonstrates more than it decides. It does all this by *engaging* – itself above all, and consequently others.[10]

The capacity of a school principal or other educational leaders to identify with a school or district (and the school or district staff to identify

with the principal or leader), therefore, and for these leaders to negotiate a shared sense of direction for the school or district with its staff,
will depend in large measure on the trajectory that determines his or
her form of participation or non-participation in the school's or district's various 'communities of practice'. Trajectories are both tempo-
ral and spatial. Individuals move in and out of communities over time
and belong to multiple communities in different places. For example,
a teacher might be a member of a community of colleagues at school
and also of a mutual support group at a district level.

From a career perspective, however, there is a degree of linearity
to leaders' trajectories in relationship to individual schools, districts,
or departments, as they negotiate their 'identities' within different
communities. Leaders tend to progress from an 'inbound' trajectory
through a 'peripheral' trajectory to become an 'insider'. In time, the
leader pursues an 'outbound' trajectory as departure from a community, such as a school, becomes imminent. If a leader moves to
another school or department or into other roles, the leader spans a
'boundary' that becomes part of the leader's 'inbound' trajectory
into a new setting or career stage. Some leaders who have spanned
the boundaries of a number of different 'communities' usually
develop richer 'inbound' trajectories when they move into new settings than those leaders with very limited 'boundary' trajectories.
Charmaine Watson who we met in the last chapter could call on her
experiences at Talisman Park to help her to move expeditiously
towards a school-wide approach to literacy at her new school,
Wayvern. At the same time, a person can follow any or all of these
trajectories with different 'communities of practice' depending on
his or her degree of involvement.

'Inbound' trajectories

'Inbound' trajectories apply to individuals who join a community
with the "prospect of becoming full participants in its practice."[11]
Their engagement may be peripheral in the beginning but in time
they expect to become an 'insider'. The following examples of
various leaders illustrates learning needs at each juncture and the
type of professional support they required at each stage.[12]

Barbara Doubleday, who recently retired as the principal of a very

large, quite complex secondary school after many years of successful leadership experiences, traced the roots of her 'inbound' trajectory to her very first teaching job at Lord Byron, with Wayne the
principal introduced in Chapter 2, and her department head Wally
in the English department. As she explained:

> I had several job offers, but I chose to go to Byron because of
> Wally and Wayne. I liked the interview; I liked the approach.
> But I particularly liked the way they interacted with me. My
> decision was based on people not on program. I really had no
> idea what I was getting into. Wally explained to me that I could
> develop some courses, which for me at that time would have
> been of interest anyway. I had already done a little bit in my
> teacher training course development. They always told me,
> however, "don't worry, you probably don't have to do that for a
> couple of years." Wally immediately gave me a senior level
> program to develop called 'Integrative Canadian Literature' – a
> pilot programme, which probably would have daunted a lot of
> people nowadays. But in those days, I felt that it was just part of
> the job expectation. If you had something given to you and it
> was big, then that was great. So, I took it and spent the summer
> developing a course.
>
> I must have read a thousand novels; that's what it felt like. In
> fact I judged right. I judged that those people would give me an
> opportunity and a big time challenge all at the same time. Now
> being an administrator, I look back at it from my present per-
> spective, and realise that at that time it was a statement of faith.
> And that was necessary for my growth. If people don't have a
> statement of faith, then I don't believe people will grow. That's
> what I have experienced.
>
> My role then throughout my career has been to demonstrate
> to others that I had the faith in them and if they make a mistake
> that I will stand by them. But they have to try. If they don't try,
> then they don't grow. It's like the lovely poem, "if you don't
> start walking, you don't go anywhere." They've got to try –
> that's an empathetical position too. You also have to have clear
> goals. I know that I have to have goals to move people, but
> within that is this huge area. Wally used to call it the 'balloon',
> structured multiplicity. It's this huge opportunity realm. You

can still have goals and work toward goals, but if you don't provide that ambiguity that allows people to work through that ambiguity, I don't think they'll ever grow.

And so throughout my career path, I have always looked for people who are willing to take a few risks, get moving, and get going. My path would have been fairly consistent at the time. I was an early head and joined into a department where it was very collegial. So, the work on collaboration was early embedded in me.

Barbara provides an example of a teacher who accepted a leadership challenge very early in her career, but a challenge balanced by support from her principal and skill development from her department head, so that she did not become overwhelmed. In a sense she was in 'flow', intellectually stretched, deeply engaged in meaningful work, but happy. As a result she brought the ideas of challenge and support to her leadership activities into her new settings as part of her 'inbound trajectory' as a leader of learning.

By way of contrast to the informal leadership opportunities Barbara talked about, Ken Sutton described the various formal leadership roles that contributed to his 'inbound trajectory'. Ken Sutton was the principal of Lord Byron in the late 1990s. Lord Byron was his third principalship. Before that he had been a department head and an assistant principal in two secondary schools. He felt his varied experiences in a number of schools enriched his 'inbound' trajectory. As he stated:

From what I've read, the height of your effectiveness (as a principal) seems to be somewhere between the five and seven years period. Then after that, it doesn't have the same dramatic rise and it tends to level out if you look at a graph in terms of your effectiveness. Going into a new setting is always rejuvenating and for me it was exciting because every school has its own sense of community, its own history, its own way of doing things, and its own ethos. It's very easy to follow into a nice rhythm and routine and just stay where you are. Whereas this forces you to meet new challenges and I learned from every single setting. It was a marvellous experience.

These examples of 'inbound trajectories' beg the question – what types of experiences do potential leaders require to help them become leaders of learning? (I return to this question in the final chapter on succession planning.) In preparation for principalship, Sutton had spent two to three years as an assistant principal in each of two schools to enrich his 'inbound' trajectory. The brevity of his stay in both cases, however, would have limited him to a 'peripheral' trajectory in each. He simply would not have had the time to negotiate an 'insider's' trajectory.

'Peripheral' trajectories

'Peripheral' trajectories may never lead to full participation but are significant to one's identity. Assistant principals in Ontario who are systematically rotated from setting to setting like Ken Sutton only have the opportunity to become part of a 'community of practice' once they are established as principals when they have a longer tenure in a school. Even then, when leaders move into new settings, they will spend a considerable amount of time on a 'peripheral trajectory' as they negotiate a new identity as an 'insider'. The larger the school, the more difficult it is to identify with, and negotiate into its communities of practice.

In Chapter 2, I introduced Wayne the 'artist', who with Garry the 'craftsman', guided the formation of a powerful learning community at Lord Byron. After Wayne's fourth year as principal at the school, the system promoted him to a supervisory role. Six months later the system moved Garry to a more traditional school to broaden his 'inbound' trajectory in preparation for his eventual promotion. Bruce Grey (a pseudonymous, composite figure), the assistant principal from a very traditional neighbouring school, replaced Wayne. Grey was thirty-four years of age and had gained a reputation as an able administrator. During Grey's three year tenure before his promotion to another school district, Byron grew in population from 900 to 2,000 students. At the same time, Grey acted almost immediately to continue the change agenda. He poured time, energy and money into a community school concept, introduced immersion programs, and supported innovations throughout the school. Staff, however, began to experience innovation overload, and mourned for the early days under Wayne's leadership. The district's intention was to maintain continuity – to appoint an innovative young principal to continue Wayne's work – but Bruce Grey never became an 'insider' and remained on a 'peripheral' trajectory throughout his tenure. In fact many staff just marginalised him and waited for his inevitable departure.

Grey's very first action as principal was to overrule the decision of a staff committee he had empowered to hire a department head. As one teacher stated, "He just didn't get it – he never understood." She told the story of how he prominently displayed a book on his desk entitled *Winning through Intimidation*. Rather than engaging in a thorough entry process before launching new innovations, he rapidly pushed his own agenda from the first day in school. Day and Bakioglu's research suggests that "Making too many changes in the first year without getting to know the school culture, staff, and community was identified by the experienced head teachers (principals) as an error."[13] But Grey was a man in a hurry. He had become the district's youngest secondary principal and as he himself admitted was "ruthlessly obsessed by goals." Staff questioned his motives and attributed many of his initiatives to his overweening desire to 'look good' to gain promotion, rather than to any aspiration to enhance the school and its program. When he did get promoted to another district, the school district belatedly assigned the former Byron 'insider' Garry to the post, but unfortunately a changing provincial context and significant personnel changes undermined his efforts to resuscitate the school's innovative structures and programs. The damage from Grey's ill-conceived appointment had been done. His ineffectiveness initiated a period of retrenchment and retreat for the school from which it never recovered. Grey's 'inbound' trajectory had not prepared him for a school such as Byron, and his values and goals were clearly incompatible with the staff he had inherited. Moreover, as 'a man in a hurry' he never took the time to understand what the school was about.

Even leaders like Garry, who are promoted from within a school, must renegotiate a new identity based on their changed relationship to the school's various communities. This suggests that leaders need to learn entry strategies that provide them with an understanding of their context before they can become an influential part of it. One of the problems of rapid turnover of leaders is that a school's staff learns to recognise this impermanence and tends to exclude them from full participation in the school as a community of practice.

Stewart Heights Secondary School[14] provides two different examples of leaders who remained on 'peripheral' trajectories for quite different reasons. Stewart Heights had evolved from a small, predominantly white and middle-class school in to a large multi-cultural, multi-racial secondary school. Bill Andrews had experience as the principal of two other secondary schools before the system appointed him to Stewart Heights. His predecessor had been very much of an 'insider' who had allowed the school to cruise along, unaware or perhaps unable to respond to the changing demographics of the school. As a result, the school retained the policies and practices of 'a village school' that were quite out of step with reality. Andrews had experience as the principal of two schools as well as serving for two years in a system-wide role in the district office. Teachers commented on his ability to use the system for the school's advantage. His considerable experience allowed him to move confidently, quickly, and energetically to shake the school out of its insularity and redirect staff members' efforts towards the interests of students and the community.

By articulating firm expectations for staff performance and student behaviour, and by demonstrating through example that change was possible, he succeeded in moving the school to a point by the end of his second year as principal where it was beginning to function as a professional learning community. He aggressively addressed the dominance of a department heads group that his predecessor had allowed to run the school. Many staff members who had felt left out of decision making welcomed Andrews's more open approach. As one teacher observed, "He's the boss guiding – whatever goes, goes. I think he likes input from us. He gets input from us but he sort of makes his own decisions. Bill (the principal) listens and then makes the decision based on what he hears, but the forum's there so we can express it." While Andrews was generally responsive to staff opinions, there was no doubt who made the final decisions and who was in charge. His agenda was clear. The teacher-centred orientation of the past must become more learner-centred to respond to Stewart Heights's diverse cultures and social groupings.

After only two years at Stewart Heights, Andrews received an appointment to a senior position at the district office. There was no time to consolidate his legacy through building leadership networks, and limited opportunity to connect with the in-coming principal and his assistants. The needs of the system clearly had superseded the needs of the school.

It was into this situation in 2000 that the board parachuted Jerry West, a new principal appointee, and two newly appointed assistant principals. As West observed, "The previous principal had had ten years' experience. Now he was here only for two years, but he came in with a certain skill set having had ten years' experience. I came in with no experience … so I had to develop some other skills … as well as running the school." The departure of Andrews's assistant principals, and their replacement by inexperienced appointees, exacerbated Jerry West's feelings of being overwhelmed and isolated. At the time of his appointment to Stewart Heights, West was just settling into his second assistant principal position after five years as the assistant in a small rural secondary school.

Despite his enthusiasm and experience as an assistant principal, he found the first eighteen months of his new role daunting. His previous experiences had not prepared him for the challenge of replacing such a high profile and indeed charismatic leader as Bill Andrews, nor how to deal with mandated external reforms. West had to deal with a staff that felt that "we are not going to have a principal come in and tell us what to do." He observed that:

> The role of the principal is dramatically different than that of the assistant principal. I've moved from more operational pieces as an assistant principal to the human resources, policy and program responsibilities of the principal. There is a whole piece of learning about where to get information from and who to rely on to make a prudent decision. It doesn't matter if you're a new teacher or a new principal – when you walk in new, it is work, building a reputation, and building trust. After 18 months, my stomach has finally stopped churning.

Like many novice principals, West had received little formal induction to the role or to his new school. He felt frustrated by the circumstances of his appointment. Only a few years before, West would have been able to count on his local superintendent or an experienced colleague to orient and mentor him. By the time he arrived at Stewart Heights, the district office had cut the number of local superintendents to reduce the district's budget, and the few senior colleagues who had not taken advantage of early retirement were themselves on overload. Although he knew that it was important for Stewart Heights to keep progressing, West felt he needed a year "just getting to understand the school." Because the school had had such a rapid turnover of principals, he also sensed that some of the staff were ready to 'outwait' him and so block or ignore any changes that he proposed. As he explained, "It's only been one plus years but teachers are coming to me already and asking how long are you going to be here?"

Unfortunately the pressure of events denied West the opportunity to negotiate an entry process that would enable him to build meaningful relationships with his school's communities of practice. His promotion had occurred at the same time as the pressure to implement the standards agenda of the provincial government was at its peak. Unlike Andrews, Jerry had limited opportunity to develop a sense of direction with his staff – his efforts were superseded by pre-packaged mandates from outside the school and its community. He explained that "as we were making our own changes, moving forward in the direction that we believed we need to go, other changes and outside pressures have been imposed on us as well. So things that you want to do have to take a back seat sometimes and that can be quite frustrating."

The early achievements of school improvement at Stewart Heights under Andrews faded quickly. Hierarchical structures, particularly the department heads group that had dominated before Andrews's arrival, reasserted its authority, and West acquiesced because he needed support to ensure the school's compliance with the government's curriculum and assessment requirements. His lack of decisiveness as a result of changing circumstances led some staff members to see him and his assistants as ineffectual. A long-serving teacher commented – "Nice people. But they can't cope. And they're not. Three rookies – they're not coping at all."

West provides an example of a leader who was not prepared for the task and was virtually abandoned by his district, left to muddle through as best he could in the face of unprecedented government changes. He had to resort to seeking support from traditional micro-political groups to ensure compliance. At the same time his inexperience left him feeling vulnerable, and unable to stand up to outside interference in his leadership of the school. West was not only 'peripheral', he and his assistants became marginalised as the school regressed to more traditional policies and practices. Conversely, Andrews made significant changes in the school, but his case demonstrates the limits of charismatic leadership. Such leaders can make short-term changes, but unless they can achieve an 'insider's' trajectory, their changes tend to be short term. This suggests that leaders can make dramatic short-term changes from the periphery, but unless they move to an 'insider's' trajectory their changes will evaporate in short order. Both Andrews and West, therefore, provide contrasting examples of leaders who remained on the periphery and failed to develop an 'insider's' trajectory from which sustained influence and change can occur, although Andrews might well have succeeded had he stayed for a few more years.

'Insider' trajectories

'Insider' trajectories grow and develop over time, as one becomes a full member of a community. It is from within communities of practice that leaders are at their most effective. Charmaine Watson moved from the periphery to an 'insider's' trajectory at Wayvern, and of course Wayne and Garry were 'insiders' at Byron, but the evidence from the *Change Over Time* study suggests that many of the leaders we studied failed to gain an 'insider's' trajectory because they continued to view their schools in hierarchical terms, rather than seeing them as webs or complex networks that linked a multiplicity of 'communities of practice'. The danger of an 'insider's' trajectory, however, is that once a person achieves 'insider' status, it is a relatively short step to becoming so encultured in the school's community of practice that they become guardians of the status quo rather than leaders of a learning community. As Ken Sutton stated in his interview, the accepted wisdom in many North American jurisdictions is that heads lose their effectiveness after their seventh or eighth year in a school. It is for this reason that principals in both the USA and Canada are routinely moved to new settings. The question remains, however, how can serving school leaders continue to learn and to grow as leaders? How can training institutions enhance the qualities and 'learnings' of incumbent heads and assistants?

New events, practices and people are certainly occasions for renegotiating one's identity but in a climate in which schools are judged
almost solely on test scores, there appears to be little incentive to do
so in those schools with higher achieving students, other than a
leader's personal desire to continue to grow professionally. The most
common complaint I hear from district officials is that they find it
very difficult to engage the leaders of what Louise Stoll and I have
called 'cruising' schools.[15] These are schools that appear effective
because of the quality of their student intake but have a limited
capacity for growth and development. Since many of these schools
have become smug and self-satisfied, it is often useful to change the
boundaries within their communities of practice to recreate some
'aliveness'. Change of personnel, alterations to the formal structures, or a change in assignments can contribute to new configurations and more energised communities. Crossing boundaries
presents challenges but also learning opportunities.

Boundary trajectories

Boundary trajectories develop as one spans and links various communities of practice. Consultants, advisors, or senior officials of
school districts develop their identities as they move from school to
school. Similarly, special education teachers within schools are often
'network' leaders because they can cross boundaries that senior
managers and department heads cannot traverse.[16] School districts
in the USA base their policies of regularly rotating principals and
assistant principals from school to school on the need for their
leaders to span boundaries, thus gaining a system's perspective.
Leaders like Ken Sutton found the experience professionally enriching. Charmaine Watson and Bill Andrews used their experiences to
provide decisive leadership in their new settings. Jerry West with his
limited and rather narrow experience actually became marginalised
at Stewart Heights. While building a leader's 'inbound' trajectory by
crossing various boundaries may contribute to their efficacy as
leaders, there is evidence that the 'revolving door' principalship
actually undermines sustainable change.[17] For example, many of
the changes introduced by Wayne and Garry at Lord Byron, and by

Bill Andrews at Stewart Heights, simply disappeared or languished after their departures.

This paradox presents a dilemma. How can a district or school meet the apparent need for their prospective leaders to have a rich 'inbound' trajectory through crossing boundaries, whilst ensuring stability and sustainability of important changes in the various settings they enter and leave? How do potential leaders learn the 'big picture' without crossing boundaries? Are there alternative routes to school leadership? Is leadership experience necessary before one becomes a teacher of others? Since boundary trajectories are linked closely to inbound trajectories, how does a potential leader experience a variety of communities of practice without disrupting the communities they traverse? I will come back to these questions of succession in the next chapter but on a final note, how does one leave a setting to pursue an 'outbound trajectory' whilst ensuring that one's legacy continues and important changes are sustained?

'Outbound' trajectories

Outbound trajectories apply to those who plan or expect to move out of a community at some time. Their participation in one community is built on where they are going next. In some cases, their outbound trajectory becomes part of their inbound trajectory in the move to a new setting. For others who are departing school leadership permanently and in increasing numbers, their 'outbound' trajectory becomes part of their entry to a second career. Leaders on an outbound trajectory need to consider their leadership legacy and attend to issues regarding the sustainability of educational change.[18] Every one of the leaders described thus far has moved on, either to retirement or to other settings. Some have left a rich legacy, and others were practically forgotten the day they walked out the door for the last time. Wayne's legacy at Lord Byron continued over time,[19] through leaders who in the early 1990s held many of the important leadership roles in the school district. At one point, Wayne and the Lord Byron experience had directly influenced 13 of the 16 secondary school principals, the district's director, two superintendents, and a number of assistant principals and consultants (advisors). Interestingly, they all followed Wayne's leadership style and profoundly influenced not just one school, but an entire school district.[20]

Before her stay at Wayvern that I have described in some detail, Charmaine Watson was principal at Talisman Park Secondary School. She had only thought consciously about her 'outbound trajectory' in her last year at Talisman Park. Upon her arrival at the school, she discovered that Talisman Park had most of the characteristics of a 'cruising' school[21] – self-satisfied and generally unaware or unwilling to address the changing nature of the school's population. It took her a few years to get most of the staff even to recognise that there were issues that they needed to address. With the support of most of the staff members and parents, however, she had not only identified the key issues for the school but was well on the way to addressing them when the district abruptly moved her, before she had a chance to consolidate her achievement. She was, as she declared, "devastated" when she was transferred after only three and a half years as principal. As a result the school rather rapidly reverted back to structures and practices that she had actively worked to alter. Her 'outbound trajectory' at Wayvern was much more successful. Charmaine herself was also a different leader at Wayvern than she had been at Talisman Park. She was more experienced, more skilful, and more focused on her outbound trajectory because she knew when she intended to retire. Wayvern School was also a very different situation to that of Talisman Park. It was a 'struggling' school that had experienced a few years of questionable leadership and its staff recognised that changes had to be made. At Wayvern she had the opportunity to put the right leaders in the right places, and to use the imminent literacy test to focus the staff on the school-wide literacy initiative described in the last chapter. She left a very rich legacy in terms of student learning and distributive leadership.

Bruce Grey's legacy of frenetic changes at Lord Byron yielded few if any lasting results. Virtually every innovation he introduced had disappeared within a few years of his departure, partly because of his technocratic style, and to a certain extent his failure to generate staff support. These were seen as purely his agenda and when he left so did any commitment. Bill Andrews's case is similar. His forceful and charismatic style meant that the very meaningful changes he initiated were wrapped up in his persona, and without him to champion the cause the school quickly reverted back to old habits. His successor, Jerry West, never really had a chance to make an imprint on the school because of external pressures and his own inexperience and ineptitude. He departed the school after three years, physically and mentally exhausted, with little to show for his efforts. Few leaders think about their 'outbound trajectory' until their time of departure and by that time they are so concentrated on the next stage of their career that they give little notice to their legacy in their previous setting. It is little wonder that teachers become jaded and cynical about educational change.

The evolution of effective leaders, therefore, requires them to *differentiate* themselves from others by developing the qualities described in Chapter 4 and acquiring the 'learnings' necessary to become those leaders of learning outlined in Chapter 5. In this chapter, the discussion of trajectories has attempted to show the patterns and challenges that leaders tend to pursue as they attempt to *integrate* into new settings or renegotiate their identity within an existing setting. As leaders successfully combine their abilities to differentiate and integrate they become much more *complex*, and therefore more capable of leading schools and districts in challenging times.

Conclusion

The metaphors we use tend to reflect the prevailing organisational template of the times. In the late nineteenth and early twentieth centuries images derived from industry permeated organisational and management theories. Traditional Public Administration, with its hierarchies and bureaucracies, reflected a mechanistic metaphor. This machine metaphor meant that managers, like engineers, created systems to ensure predictability of results by designing structures such as assembly lines, carefully delineated job descriptions, rigid product specifications, and detailed accountability relationships. McDonald's still operates on this mechanistic metaphor. This metaphor has manifested itself in education through mandates, guidelines, and detailed policies and procedures.

The 'market' metaphor of the 1990s reflects New Public Management's focus on competition, the 'bottom line' defined in quantitative terms, performance accountability tied to results, and an empowered consumer. By their very nature, markets are built on an adversarial relationship in which both the buyer and seller or customer or supplier hope to gain advantage. Moreover, markets are inherently inequitable. While they are the best way society has found to produce wealth, they are not particularly good at distributing its rewards. Markets produce winners and losers and the latter is usually the poor, the disenfranchised, and the marginalised. Educational policies based on the market have further undermined equity in society by producing schools for the 'haves' and schools for the 'have nots' in many western educational jurisdictions.

Influenced by the success of the internet and other globalised networks and the failings of unfettered markets, the metaphor of the web has become a widely held way to describe organisations and other economic and social aspects of society. This metaphor guides our understanding of learning communities and suggests a definition of freedom that is quite different from the 'market' metaphor. In the "market era, freedom is defined as autonomy. One is free to the extent one is not dependent or beholden to another," and in a web "One's freedom is secured by belonging, not by belongings. To belong, one needs access. With access, one can enjoy the freedom that goes with inclusivity. Freedom is found in shared relationships rather than isolation."[22] As Rifkin explains, "Markets are based on mistrust, networks on trust. Markets are based on the pursuit of self-interest, networks on shared interest. Markets are arms' length transactions, networks are intimate relationships. Markets are competitive, networks are cooperative."[23]

If Traditional Public Administration produced the 'organisation man' and New Public Administration has produced 'technocrats'[24] and 'false heroes'[25], then networks require leaders who are 'engagers', connectors, and facilitators of "the emergence of novelty." "This means creating the conditions rather than giving directions, and using the power of authority to empower others. Being a leader means creating a vision; it means going where nobody has gone before. It also means enabling the community as a whole to create something new. Facilitating emergence means facilitating creativity."[26] To extend the 'web' metaphor and this view of leadership further, the next chapter develops the *Leadership for Mortals* model introduced at the beginning of this book into a systemic plan for leadership development and sustainability.

Notes

1 Capra. F. (2002). *The Hidden Connections: A science for sustainable living*. New York: Anchor Books.
2 Ibid, p. 111.
3 Wenger, E. (1998). *Communities of Practice*. Cambridge: Cambridge University Press, p. 149.
4 Ibid, p. 149.
5 Ibid, p. 188.
6 Ibid, p. 154.
7 Ibid, p. 152.
8 Mintzberg, H. (2004). *Managers not MBAs: A hard look at the soft practice of managing and management development*. San Francisco, CA: Berrett-Koehler Publishers, p. 141.
9 Ibid, p. 141.
10 Ibid, p. 143.
11 Ibid, p. 154.
12 From *Change Over Time* study; op. cit.
13 Day, C. and Bakioglu, H. (1996). 'Development and disenchantment in the professional lives of head teachers', in J. Goodsen and A. Hargreaves (eds), *Teachers' Professional Lives*, London: Falmer, pp. 205–17; p. 210.
14 The Stewart Heights case is taken from Spencer's study, although I have renamed it to avoid confusion with other work emerging from the project.
15 Stoll and Fink (1996) op. cit.
16 Senge, P.M., Kleiner, A., Roberts, C., Ross R., Roth, G. and Smith B. (1999). *The Dance of Change*. New York: Doubleday.
17 Macmillan, R. (2000). 'Leadership succession, culture of teaching, and educational change', in N. Bascia and A. Hargreaves (eds), *The Sharp Edge of Educational Change*. London: Falmer Press.
18 Hargreaves, A. and Fink, D. (2003). 'Sustaining leadership', in B. Davies and J. West-Burnham (eds), *Handbook of Educational Leadership and Management*. London: Pearson Education.
19 See Fink, D. (2000). *Good Schools, Real Schools: Why school reform doesn't last*. New York: Teachers' College Press.
20 Ibid.
21 Stoll and Fink (1996) op. cit.
22 Rifkin, J. (2004). *The European Dream: How Europe's future is quietly eclipsing the American dream*. New York: Tarcher/Penguin, p. 192.
23 Ibid, p. 193.
24 Pitcher, op. cit.
25 Saul (1993) op. cit.
26 Capra (2004) op. cit., p. 122.

7 Succession[1]

As I write this final chapter, it is autumn in Ontario. It is my favourite season. The trees are beautiful shades of red, yellow and orange, the days are warm and the evenings cool, the corn is fresh and sweet, and the tomatoes taste like tomatoes. Almost hourly Canada Geese fly over my house in their perfect 'V' formations as they head to a warmer climate. They have perfected leadership succession – whenever the leader of the 'V' gets tired, it falls back and another takes its place. This pattern continues as they make their way 1,500 miles to the southern USA.

If only human organisations could plan as efficiently and effectively. With the high leadership turnover in education described in the introduction, leadership succession should be a topic of more than passing interest. Not only are there not sufficient numbers of potential leaders coming forward as the much smaller generation 'X' replaces the 'baby boom' generation, but, as the foregoing six chapters have indicated, those that do seek leadership opportunities must address significantly different challenges from the leaders that they will replace. Ironically, a search of the internet produces a plethora of business related references and only a few that connect to education or to the public service. It appears that both are, for the most part, still tied to a traditional leadership replacement model rather than to a leadership development approach.

Fulmer and Conger indicate that business leaders in the future

> will need greater technological literacy, a sophisticated knowledge of the global marketplaces, fluency in multiple cultures, entrepreneurial skills, extensive networks of varied relationships, changing leadership skills, the ability to lead in increasingly 'delayered', 'disaggregated' and 'virtual' organizations.[2]

With the change of a word or two, this description applies to the public sector, including education, but judging by the volume of business literature on the topic of succession management, the public sector has much to learn from the private sector.

The private sector

Rothwell describes the traditional private sector method of succession management as a process that "helps ensure the stability of tenure of personnel."[3] In practice this means that businesses try to match individuals to statically defined positions. "This approach, however, is outdated and conflicts with the rapidly changing needs of today's organizations."[4] Contemporary approaches to 'succession management' in business take a much broader view on the succession processes, and now focus on 'leaders' learnings' like those described by Fulmer and Conger, rather than on specific jobs.[5] The National Academy of Public Administration defines succession management as

> a deliberate and systemic effort to project leadership requirements, identify a pool of high potential candidates, develop leadership competencies in those candidates through intentional learning experiences, and then select leaders from among the pool of potential leaders.[6]

The aim of succession management, therefore, is to match an organisation's present available talent to its future talent needs, or as Rothwell succinctly expresses it, "having the right people at the right places at the right time to do the right things."[7] He explains that it is an important tool of organisational learning because it should ensure that:

> the lessons of organizational experience – what is sometimes called institutional memory – will be preserved and combined with reflection on that experience to achieve continuous improvement in work results. Stated another way, (it) is a way to ensure the continued cultivation of leadership and intellectual talent and manage the critically knowledge assets of organization.[8]

With the impending retirements of 40 to 50 per cent of the existing leaders in the private sector, organisations have identified succession management as a problem that they need to address urgently.[9] Early retirements, downsizing, and reorganisations have created critical shortages of middle and top leaders in the business community for the immediate future.[10] To attend to this pressing problem, business observers contend that organisations must embark on systemic succession management programs to replace departing leaders.[11] While different authors emphasise various aspects of succession processes, there appears to be considerable agreement on the following principles of effective succession management.[12]

- The succession process should be directly connected to the strategic purposes and values of the organisation.

- The chief executive of the organisation should champion the organisation's succession management.

- Line managers must take ownership of succession management so that staff support the process.

- Potential and existing leaders should be judged on their ability to learn and to develop the learning of others in the organisation.[13]

- Managers should be held accountable for human resources reviews and implementing their outcomes.

- Succession management is fully co-ordinated with the corporate human resources system and strategy.

- The succession process is simple and focused on people not technology.

- Succession management is tailored to the organisation's unique needs, culture and history.

- Succession management drives leadership development programs.

The best companies search for potential leaders, and expend considerable time, energy and money to prepare them for future leadership. By way of contrast, the public sector, including education in most western countries, with notable exceptions appears unable or unwilling to invest in leadership succession.

The public service

Although scholars and senior public servants in most western countries are becoming increasingly concerned regarding the recruitment and development of future leaders in the public service, it is becoming an increasingly urgent issue as the 'baby boom' generation moves on.[14] By 2005, for example, 70 per cent of the senior managers in the US public service will be eligible for retirement, "causing unique challenges for numerous agencies in maintaining leadership continuity, institutional memory and workforce experience."[15] Similar patterns are reported in Canada[16] and Australia.[17] In recent years, a combination of regulatory, budgetary and collective agreement restrictions have limited the flexibility of the public sector to recruit and develop new leaders. These factors when combined with attacks on the dedication and efficacy of the public service by politicians, corporate leaders, and the press, suggest that it is not surprising that public servants in many western jurisdictions are feeling disgruntled and "marginalised".[18] As a result, this sector finds it increasingly difficult to compete with business for people with leadership potential. Schall has identified the following problems that particularly affect public sector efforts at succession planning:

- that current leaders are reluctant to take up the succession task;

- that the assumption has been made that succession issues are beyond the scope of leaders' work;

- that there is confusion on the nature of succession management;

- that there is a difficulty in planning for succession in the face of a shifting political environment, restrictive regulations, and budgetary and personnel constraints.[19]

Jackson[20] suggests that the two sectors tend to approach the entire process of succession management quite differently. The public sector is passive, allowing candidates to emerge, whereas more forward-thinking private sector organisations actively recruit and encourage potential leaders. The public sector looks to the short term, is much more informal, and tends to look for replacements for existing roles. The private sector generally looks at the long term to determine the kinds of leadership skills and aptitudes needed in the future. Jackson contends that the public sector focuses on competencies based on the existing roles, whereas the private sector is more interested in people who have 'learned how to learn' and are sufficiently flexible to adjust to changing business situations.

Perhaps the most significant difference is the value each of these segments of society places on succession management. The public sector views succession management as a 'cost' to the organisation. Conversely, in a knowledge society, the more progressive elements of the private sector view personnel development as an organisational 'asset'. In fact, some of the most progressive businesses object to using the term 'asset' because it implies ownership of people. As one Canadian CEO stated, "People are not the most important asset of a company. They are the company. Everything else is an asset."[21] This fundamental value difference contributes significantly to the development of succession management in the private sector, and the relative immobility of the public sector to plan and manage succession effectively.

Educational sector

Educational systems tend to follow the public sector model. Educational researchers have provided advice on recruitment and selection processes,[22] training and preparation programs[23] and guidelines for structuring socialisation experiences for school administrators[24] as well as systemic rotation of leaders to ensure a breadth of experience.[25] Macmillan's study of secondary principals in Ontario provides insight into the process of leader adaptation to new settings and the effects on school staff. Overall, the available research provides limited and conflicting views on the practice of leadership succession in schools.

Modelling the practices of the best businesses, school systems need to define leadership roles flexibly in terms of what will be required in the future rather than by limiting role descriptions to existing competencies.[26] In addition, the involvement of senior policy leaders in the processes of succession management is as important in school districts as in private businesses. Perhaps the most significant finding from the business literature is that the succession plans must be "tailored to the organization's unique needs, culture and history: there are no quick fixes."[27] This is also true of schools and school districts. As we have found in curriculum, testing, school organisation and leadership trajectories – 'one size does not fit all'. Wenger's concept of trajectories[28] discussed in Chapter 6, however, provides individuals, schools and school districts with a useful guide around which they can develop succession management processes that will produce a coherent approach to identifying, developing, and promoting school and district leadership over time.

Trajectories and succession management

Trajectories enable us to describe career paths through both time and space as careers evolve – sometimes in a linear fashion as described in the last chapter, or occasionally following multiple trajectories simultaneously. The following discussion is drawn, in part, from insights gained through interviews for the *Change Over Time* study that focused on issues of leadership and leadership succession.

Nurturing a leader's inbound trajectory

To initiate each interview, researchers invited respondents to talk about the experiences that had shaped their decision to become a teacher and influenced their views on education. A pattern emerged among those teachers who went on to assume leadership roles or had achieved positions of leadership within their schools or school districts. In all cases, they had experienced:

- the opportunity to undertake significant and challenging activities early in their careers that 'stretched' them intellectually and professionally;

- leadership development opportunities that enabled them to meet these challenges;

- supportive mentors who assisted them as they met their challenges;

- the opportunity to observe and learn from powerful models of successful leadership (and from some negative examples);

- feedback on their performance that was honest and constructive (although not always positive).

Like Barbara Doubleday in the previous chapter, who faced the challenge of developing a Canadian Studies curriculum for senior students, some others reported similar engaging opportunities. For example, Ken Sutton explained how the school system gave him unique chances to contribute:

> I was always interested in innovation and change and even as a department head way back when. I had the opportunity to initiate a lot of new programs in the system that simply didn't exist before. I'm proud of the fact that I chaired the region-wide committee on a World Religions course. The second one that I chaired was a course on Future Studies. It was highly successful in the mid-1970s. In fact we had a region-wide Futures fair where all the teachers who were teaching Future Studies had their students do major projects. It was like a science fair where it was open to the community and media and we had the TV cameras there and so on.

Bill, a leading special educator in one of the districts we investigated, described his early challenges as a novice teacher and the role of his mentor, his principal Ron.

> Ron was simply amazing because I think that people in our profession need to be recognised for whatever they do. Ron was really good at that. He'd pick up on little things. You'd get a note that said "thanks for a great job, I saw you out in the hall talking to that kids and that was really good", or "thanks for your involvement" in this activity or that. So when he needed to make a point with you about something else, perhaps an area for improvement, you were on the same level. It wasn't somebody from above saying, "No, this is wrong!" You accepted it more. He was really good at polishing people.
>
> He'd take somebody that was rough like me. I was a rookie teacher. I was raw. I didn't know the things that maybe other teachers knew about special education. But he was really good

at polishing raw material like me by saying, "OK. The core is good. What we've got to do is finish the edges." He gave me a really good start because he said, "If you need to take a risk to do something that's different and you know why you want to do it, then do it, and stick to your guns and I'll support you," and that's what I did for eight years. There was on-going communication so that you really felt that you were part of a team. I always look at those eight years as being the basis of building what I eventually evolved into as far as my commitment to special education was concerned.

Joyce provides a third example. She not only became a well-respected principal but at one point in her career she was the first female president of the district's teachers' union.

I think what happened for me at Lord Byron was that I learned how to learn. I learned that I had to do some of that for myself. I developed a lot of confidence. I learned a lot from Wayne. He and I would be there early in the morning and he would walk into my office with an article and say, "you might like to read this." That was so important to me and we were a big staff. There were a lot of people in that school. But to walk in early in the morning and watch who is there and talk to the young people that were there, and say "what do you thing about this?" I often did that as principal. But the whole learning process was the key one. The opportunities to share and to learn new things together were the things I really felt kept me moving and kept us moving at that time.

Ironically, these potential leaders also learned and gained confidence by dealing with some negative leadership examples. As Joyce remarked:

I learned what a waste of time it is for example to have people working against a principal, which is what we did with Bruce. It was just so much energy that year trying to get Bruce to stop doing something, instead of going ahead and doing the stuff that we should have been doing anyway. But it became a kind of game. It is such a waste of time for people to get caught up in that. And I feel for people now who have to be in that. So, I learned that.

In a similar vein, Bill commented on his move to another school:

I've also worked with people that were the exact opposite (to Ron). They didn't want to listen. You were told, "This is what you do and don't ask me why, just do it." Those were really hard years. I went through one administrator at Oak Hills that worked that way and there was very little discussion that went on. The only time that I heard from him was when there was a problem and he needed help. He needed somebody to fix something. I found that very difficult because I had never experienced that before in an administrator.

The leaders who identified the potential of Ken, Joyce, and Bill provided them with modelling and mentoring as well as the challenges and support to achieve success and gain confidence. As Rosabeth Moss Kanter[29] explains, confidence is contagious and crucial to leadership success:

Confidence consists of positive expectations for favourable outcomes. Confidence influences the willingness to invest – to commit money, time, reputation, emotional energy, or other resources – or to withhold or hedge investment. This investment, or its absence, shapes the ability to perform.

Their leaders and mentors obviously recognised the willingness of these people in their formative years to learn, take risks, accept challenges, receive criticism, and work hard to improve their craft, and considered that encouraging and facilitating the professional growth of these potential leaders to be an important part of their leadership roles.

All of these successful leaders had demonstrated early on that they would become consummate professional teachers, but would they become effective leaders? It is a gigantic leap from doing the work oneself to getting work done through others. The challenge of identification of potential leaders, therefore, is to determine who can make this leap from successful 'doers' to accomplished 'negotiators' who hold the lives of other adults in their hands. Ironically, one of the most perplexing discoveries of people who move from the role of 'doer' to that of a 'leader' is that they become less free to act.[30] In my own experience, I discovered that the greater my organisational responsibilities, the less free I became. As a classroom teacher I looked at my principals and thought of all their formal power, but didn't realise that to get things done they were dependent on the staff, their peers, senior officials and the politicians in the district. One of my former bosses used to talk about 'golden handcuffs'. He felt that to accomplish anything worthwhile he had to get permission from a wide array of individuals and groups within and outside the educational system. He had to get the unions, the school board and his leadership team all to agree before he could even think of moving forward. The challenge for those responsible for recruiting potential leaders is to determine who among the 'doers' have the ability, the patience, and the determination to become leaders of learning.

Identification and recruitment of potential leaders

In the cases of Ken, Joyce, and Bill, a leader identified potential and encouraged their professional growth. Identification of potential leaders in education, however, is certainly not an exact science. Traditionally, potential leaders have signalled their interest in leadership roles by applying for posted or advertised positions, or existing leaders have encouraged subordinates to seek promotion and supported their applications. As the previous discussion on the public service indicates, the process is somewhat 'hit and miss'. While responsibility for identifying and recruiting potential leaders depends on the governance structure of each educational setting, it is very clear that the psychological and financial support of the governing authorities contributes significantly to producing capable educational leaders for any school jurisdiction.[31] Baltzell and Dentler[32] contend that the extent to which a school system invests in the preparation of its principals is a key ingredient of a quality system. A major reason for the perceived crisis in quality and quantity of educational leaders in many jurisdictions, therefore, is the failure of many school districts and Local Education Authorities over the past decades to invest in leadership identification, recruitment, and preparation, and as a result they do not have a qualified pool of candidates from which to choose when openings occur.

When J.W. Singleton, my former Director,[33] visited schools he always asked the principal "who are your best performers and who are your worst?" Then he would challenge the principal with the questions of "what are you doing to develop your best, and what are you doing to change or get rid of the poorest?" He expected, indeed demanded, that principals actively develop leaders as well as attend to 'deadwood'. J.W. believed so strongly in the importance of leadership that he convinced the school district to invest in a leadership program at a time in the late 1960s when such an idea was considered frivolous in other districts in Ontario. Candidates had to be identified by their principals and proceed through a selection process to even get to attend. I remember my first session in which the course leaders gave all 32 of us course participants 15 books on educational subjects such as leadership, educational philosophy, curriculum development and teaching strategies. The program led by accomplished leaders within the system combined both the theoretical and practical aspects of leadership. All the system's senior leaders, including J.W. himself, took an active part in the program, and made sure we realised how important our development was to the system. This 'grow-your-own' philosophy perpetuated the attitude that to become a leader in Halton was a worthy goal, and that to get there we must achieve a high standard of excellence. Sadly, in the late 1990s, the leadership program in Halton was eliminated for budget reasons and only recently resuscitated. Interestingly, the system has had to rely increasingly on importing leaders from outside. Changing times and false economies have resulted in a serendipitous 'fill-the-job' philosophy, instead of the 'grow-your-own' approach that required all leaders in the system to identify and encourage potential leaders.

While, as I have already indicated, identification of potential leaders is an inexact science, I offer the following questions about potential leadership candidates as an initial guide to determining who should be recruited for leadership roles:

- Does this person genuinely like and respect the students?

- Is this person a dedicated and proficient teacher?

- Is this person committed to learning for *all* students?

- Does this person operate from a life affirming set of values and have the courage of his or her convictions?

- Has this person initiated professional growth activities to enhance his or her personal 'tool kit'?

- Has this person the intellectual and relational potential to master the meta-learnings for leadership?

- Does the person have the organisational skills to manage a school or a department?

- Does this person relate well to colleagues? To parents? To superiors in the organisation?

- Does this person have a tolerance for ambiguity?

Leadership development

Once an organisation has identified its potential leaders, it must find ways to attend to their development. Mintzberg[34] has identified five general approaches to leadership development that apply in business and are applicable in education:

- 'Sink or swim' is the least expensive approach in the short run, and by far the most prevalent approach to leadership development in education. It identifies leaders and then places them in leadership roles, and lets the person 'sink or swim'. Since leadership development in education is usually considered to be a 'cost' not an 'asset', schools and school districts find it less costly in the short term to advertise a position then hire and hope that a person works out, than to invest in expensive leadership development processes. The long-term costs of this approach, while hard to quantify, are significant. Jerry West,[35] who followed the charismatic Bill Andrews at Stewart Heights, provides an example of the costs of the 'sink or swim' approach. He arrived at the school with little preparation, little support, and at a time of major educational change. In short order, the school's staff reversed Andrews's two years of effort to move the school out of its insularity, and expended a great deal of energy on internal dissent. As a result, the school never seized the opportunity to colonise external reforms for the benefit of its students, and Jerry himself suffered both emotionally and physically from his ordeal.

- *'Moving, mentoring and monitoring'* can exist where there is a general consensus in the business literature that rotating potential leaders through a number of leadership experiences provides a variety of challenges that encompass the spectrum of the company's activities and supplies the neophyte leader with the greatest opportunity for learning. McCall found that prospective business leaders agreed with this approach because it gave them the opportunity to first witness experienced leaders dealing with complex issues, and then to address such matters themselves with the support of their mentors.[36] He provides two rules of leadership development – firstly, leadership development is a personal responsibility, and secondly,

> challenge can be provided to encourage this self-development, notably by rotating people through a series of challenging jobs that stretch their abilities: from managing a start-up to learn about 'providing strong direction in the face of ambiguity', to managing the turnaround of an existing business to learn about 'overcoming resistance and incompetence'.[37]

The educational literature is quite mixed on the practice of the systemic rotation of leaders. Aquila and Boesse[38] contend that a predictable rotation of leaders is necessary to their development. Certainly, one of our *Change Over Time* respondents, Ken Sutton, felt that his multiple moves had added to his leadership abilities:

> If I were to change schools tomorrow, then I would be able to go into the new school much more comfortably with my ability to be a principal. I would be able to assess more quickly what I believe a school should be about, to be able to talk with other people within the building what the school should be about. Take a look at the reforms that need to be implemented as we go along and move more quickly to making effective changes that we felt were necessary for our school.

MacMillan's research, however, looked at predictable principals' rotations from a school's perspective and concluded, that "the policy of regularly rotating principals within a system is a flawed one. When leadership succession is regular and routine, teachers are likely to build resilient cultures which inoculate them against the effects of succession."[39] The dilemma in education, therefore, is to determine ways to help potential leaders to experience the kind of multiple learning opportunities that moving from school to school seems to provide, while ensuring some degree of continuity and stability for each school. The important ingredient that makes such moves successful appears to be the opportunity to connect on an on-going basis with a capable mentor who helps the potential leader to reflect on practice, and provides constructive performance monitoring. As Raelin argues, "moving alone leaves the learning to the individual, whereas moving with mentoring turns it into a social process, which can make it more effective."[40] McCall supports this view[41] and reports that having "a good boss seemed to matter most in a manager's first supervisory job and in big scope jobs." Perhaps the answer in education is to view assistant principals as principals in training, and facilitate their moving on a cyclical basis, while principals contract to remain in a school for a minimum of five to seven years. Alternatively, a lateral move within an organisation allows a potential leader to gain experience while ensuring a degree of organisational stability.

- *'Spray and pray'* is an approach which refers to the practice of credentialing leaders through leadership development courses offered by school districts, universities and private consulting groups. From a system's point of view, these often uncoordinated courses vary widely in efficacy, tending to stress teaching over learning, and offering generic answers to contextually based issues. As Mintzberg has observed, "deep managing and deep learning depend on personal engagement, not just on a detached expertise that 'knows better.' So managers learn most profoundly when they have significant responsibility for all aspects of the learning process, including its design."[42] He concludes after years of teaching management courses for potential leaders that "setting out to create leaders in a classroom, whether in a short programs or full degrees, too often creates hubris. People leave believing they have been anointed."[43]

- *Learning in action* is positioned somewhere between the context based 'moving, mentoring and monitoring' and the decontextualised course work of 'spray and pray', and involves potential leaders in field projects and activities followed by serious reflection that creates a learning laboratory for leaders. Schools and school districts have often organised potential leaders into problem-solving committees to address system problems. I can remember spending hours on a committee with other prospective leaders to find better ways of reporting to parents. This and similar projects were invariably add-ons to the normal workload and we focused more on getting the job done to help the system than reflecting on our own leadership development. Mintzberg concluded in his critique of action learning that "learning is not doing: it is reflection on doing. And reflecting is not an escape but an essential part of the management process – and probably its weakest part in today's hyper world."[44]

- *Corporate academies* display an increasing trend in the business world for large corporations to establish academies that provide co-ordinated, contextualised leadership development that focuses on developing leadership potential to ensure a continuing supply of quality leaders. Such companies as Boeing, General Electric, Motorola, and even McDonald's have adopted this practice. Perhaps the closest educational equivalent is the National College for School Leadership (NCSL) in the UK, although various states and school districts support leadership assessment centres and development programs like the Halton Leadership Course I referred to previously. The NCSL not only provides courses at its Nottingham headquarters, but also has developed satellite 'colleges' and networked learning communities that provide programs for school leaders based on their career needs and certification requirements. While expensive, the urgent need for educational leaders suggests that such academies may be the wave of the future. They assess leadership potential, and also provide co-ordinated, contextualised programs that are customised to a leader's career trajectory.

The idea of trajectories, as discussed in Chapter 6, suggests that some models are more useful at different stages of a leader's career. For example, newly identified leaders would benefit from the moving, mentoring, monitoring model, whereas a long-serving principal might profit more from short courses and degree work. Much of the theory involved in course work becomes more meaningful when tied to experience.[45] Leadership development requires a judicious blending of all these approaches, but they must be tied to an individual's career stages, learning needs, system requirements, and boundaries.

Crossing boundaries

One of the most important aspects of potential leaders' 'inbound' trajectory is their support network. As leaders' careers progress, they will cross many boundaries from supportive 'communities of practice' to organisations in which they will remain on the periphery for uncomfortable periods of time. In these situations, leaders' support networks and their own 'learnings' will determine whether they become 'insiders' and reach a position to lead a school effectively. My own accession to principal of Watson High School provides an example of boundary spanning.

When I was appointed principal of Watson High School, I had to cross two boundaries; one was the political boundary of the North Area that was dominated by Dan Ford, the area's superintendent, and the other was into the school itself. To both Dan and the school staff I was quite suspect. My appointment as principal at Watson High School meant that I was on a 'peripheral' trajectory in relationship to both the school and the North Area of the district. In each case, I was very much on the outside. My reputation as an outspoken critic of conventional approaches to secondary education, and as a fairly high profile leader of one of Ontario's most innovative and renowned – or to many, notorious – 'beacon' schools had preceded me. If I had remained on the periphery, the staff of Watson would have marginalised me and Dan Ford would have made my ability to represent the school effectively very difficult.

While my experience and academic preparation had impressed my superiors in the school system who had selected me as a principal, I was totally unprepared for my first interview with Dan Ford.

For an hour (it seemed like an eternity), Ford confessed all of my real and imagined sins, those of my colleagues, and even those of my predecessor at Watson. For once in my life I kept my mouth shut, got out of his office as fast as I could, and called my former principal at Lord Byron, Wayne, who I introduced in Chapter 2 of this book. Wayne, my mentor, and Lord Byron were powerful parts of my 'inbound trajectory'. Wayne, who knew the system very well, and had a unique insight into people within it, advised me to 'shape up' my new supervisor. He explained that Ford was a superb administrator; he liked order, efficiency, promptness, and a well-developed paper trail. Over the course of my first year I made sure my reports were on his desk before any other school principal's, that they were more complete, better written, and exceeded even his expectations. I made sure his visits to the school were orchestrated to ensure he saw an orderly and well run operation. I also discovered that my predecessor had dealt with him by finding reasons to keep him out of the school as much as possible, so I decided to find reasons to include him in everything.

Interestingly, he turned out to be much more interested in good education than I had thought originally, and a very valuable advocate for the school and for me. When I applied to become a superintendent a few years later, he was my finest supporter. This was a success story because I had a support system, and superb mentoring in my 'inbound trajectory' that enabled me to negotiate a new relationship with Ford, and to build a 'community of practice' with him and his colleagues that benefited the school. The moral of this story for new leaders is to build a support system inside and outside of their own setting. Leaders, especially principals, can be very lonely, and they need all the second opinions, sober second thoughts, and words of encouragement they can get.

Operating from the periphery

When leaders enter a new setting they must negotiate their identity from a peripheral trajectory. Even people promoted from within an organisation must renegotiate their identity within the school's various communities of practice because they have now assumed a new role. For example, Janice Burnley, who had spent three years as the assistant principal at Lord Byron and had functioned from an 'insider's' trajectory, had had to renegotiate her identity after she became the school's principal when Ken Sutton retired. She almost automatically moved to a 'peripheral' trajectory with Ken no longer on the scene. In her first year as principal, Janice wisely followed the lead of the 'outbound' principal and did not initiate much that was new. She spent her first year renegotiating her identity and working to reconnect with staff as an 'insider'. In certain contextual circumstances, however, new leaders may have to act more precipitously. Elsewhere, my colleague Louise Stoll and I[46] have developed a typology to illustrate the principle that different contexts require different leadership strategies. This typology looks at schools on two dimensions – their effectiveness, and their capacity to initiate, implement and sustain important changes. It describes five types of schools:

- a *moving* school is effective and has the capacity to change. The challenge for the leaders of a moving school is to maintain its momentum.[47]

- a *cruising* school is one that appears effective because the students attain well on external tests, but the school has not the capacity to change, and is therefore not contributing as well as it might to student learning. Such schools usually are in more affluent areas. The quality of the student intake masks significant problems in the teaching–learning processes of the school. The first challenge for leadership of a cruising school is to get the teaching staff and often the community to recognise that there are problems.

- a *struggling* school is one that has the will to change and the capacity to change, but is not considered effective. It is often confused with a *sinking* school and challenged prematurely by external agencies. Struggling schools, however, do need considerable outside support to build upon a genuine desire to improve.

- a *sinking school* is neither effective nor capable of change. It requires radical surgery. A new leader will often face student and teacher discipline issues, low morale, divisiveness, and poor student results. Sinking schools are like a team on a 40 game losing streak – they expect to lose, and lack the confidence to reverse the negative spiral.[48]

- a *strolling* school is internally quite uneven because aspects of the school are effective, but in total the school is underperforming. Many secondary schools fit this description. Some departments may be excellent, some mediocre, and others quite poor. As a school, change is occurring but very slowly.

Leaders of struggling and sinking schools may have to act quickly to reverse the 'doom loop',[49] and try to create a few 'quick wins' and build staff confidence that they can tackle the larger problems. Regardless of school type, however, some version of a planned entry process helps new leaders to understand a school's culture, personnel, history, micro-politics, demographics and ethos. In crisis situations, leaders may have to lead from the periphery, but the evidence from the *Change Over Time* study suggests that leaders who make the effort and take the time to understand and move to an 'insider's' trajectory within the school's community of practice have a more lasting effect on the direction of the school. As Wenger and his colleagues state "good community design requires an insider's perspective to lead the discovery of what the community is about" and only an insider "can know who the real players are and their relationships."[50]

Upon my arrival at Watson, I spent a great deal of time in the September and October of my first year following a carefully developed entry process. I interviewed every staff member to get some insight into personal goals, ambitions, and perspectives on the school, and what they were looking for in a school principal. I also spent time with parents in small groups, community leaders, service clubs, church leaders and anyone else that could give me insight into the history and culture of the school. I studied the school's achievement and attendance data, demographic information for both students and teachers, and in general tried to get a grasp of the school's context. It became evident to me from this entry process that the teachers, with a few notable exceptions, believed that Watson's students were incapable of dealing with challenging academic work because they came from rural or working-class backgrounds. Turning this attitude around was my major leadership challenge.

In relatively short order, staff members began to include me in informal activities. I also learned that my new staff members were not unhappy to see my predecessor depart. A brilliant but somewhat moody man, he had made some major changes to the school with little staff involvement. For example, he rather arbitrarily replicated the Lord Byron timetable, department structure, and flexible staffing patterns without the Watson staff's approval, or even its understanding of the purposes of this organisation. What was 'best' practice at Lord Byron, turned out to be questionable practice at Watson. In the process, he demoted four department heads and promoted younger and more innovative people to take their places. The displaced department heads, however, remained on staff. I resolved to spend my first year building relationships and trying to bind up the wounds, so I let my assistant principals run the day-to-day operations. I began to engage each of the former heads in leadership activities, and tried to discover ways to rebuild their feelings of self-esteem. Now I know that this is not as exciting as heroically raising test scores, but these people were still teaching students, and disengaged, hurting teachers are not conducive to sustaining enhanced student achievement over time. By Christmas of my first year I was incrementally moving from a 'peripheral' to an 'insider's' trajectory. If I could negotiate an identity as an 'insider', then I could challenge the prevailing ethos that the students were incapable of rigorous academic work. Then I did something really stupid.

I had helped to write the district's policy on teacher appraisal. My colleagues and I had based it on the best research available, and developed a policy with the purpose of promoting teachers' professional growth. It involved a pre-conference before a principal's visit(s) to a classroom, the collection of data on areas that the head and teacher had agreed upon in the pre-conference, and a post-conference in which the principal and teacher discussed the visit(s) and developed a plan for further professional growth. After three months of 'entry', my urge for action got the better of me. I thought it was time to get this school moving and teacher appraisal would be the vehicle.

Where to start? At the introductory staff meeting when the departing principal had introduced me to the Watson staff, a history teacher named Jeff who I had met previously at regional meetings for history teachers had greeted me like a 'long-lost' friend, and effusively expressed his pleasure that I would be his new principal. Since Jeff seemed very supportive of me, and a history teacher as well, it made sense to me to start with him because I was not well practised in the various components of the new assessment system. Jeff and I had a pre-conference; I visited his classroom three times; I collected data, and then we had a post-conference. We talked for 15 minutes about his lessons and what I had seen. Jeff was a traditional 'stand in the front of the class and lecture and question' type of teacher. He was well prepared and the students were responsive. I felt the lessons lacked imagination and tended to be rather dull so I began to tell him of all the 'amazing' ways I had engaged students at Lord Byron,[51] and put together a folder of materials I thought he would find useful.

When he left I felt great – I was a master of this process, and I had really seemed to light a spark under my 'friend' Jeff. Within thirty minutes, the head of Jeff's department was in my office and asked me, "what did you do to Jeff?" I replied that we had just completed a 'text-book' example of teacher appraisal. The department head responded that when he asked Jeff how things had gone with Dean, Jeff's answer was "he sure kicked my ass." In spite of my best efforts over the next three years, Jeff froze me out. For him and his 'community of practice' I was not just on the periphery, I was marginalised. My unfortunate relationship with Jeff delayed my efforts to move from the 'periphery' to an 'insider's' trajectory by at least six months. The obvious moral of this story is to make haste slowly.

From the 'periphery' to the 'inside'

In my third year as principal I felt that the staff, with the exception of Jeff and his small network, had accepted me as an 'insider'. As Wenger has explained, 'insider' trajectories grow and develop over time as one becomes a full member of a community. As my situation demonstrates, the length of time to negotiate this trajectory depends on the person and the context. Certainly the fact that Watson was a relatively small secondary school (750 students and 50 staff), and that my predecessor was quite unpopular had both helped me to negotiate my 'insider's' trajectory. From this position, with the support and engagement of 95 per cent of the staff we initiated a major outdoor education program, turned the school cafeteria into a learning situation, and contributed to the design, construction, and opening of a new school building.

Perhaps my most significant move was to take a regular daily teaching assignment. I felt I had to demonstrate that Watson students could be challenged and still succeed. When I left the school a number of my former colleagues told me that my teaching had been my most important contribution to the school because it had not only cemented my 'insider's' status, but more importantly, I had helped the teachers to raise their collective expectations for student learning.

The success of a leader's entry into a new setting and eventual move to an 'insider's' trajectory, therefore, depends in large measure on the expectations of the leader's subordinates, the expectations that district officials or school governors hold for their new leader, and the new leader's own expectations. Hill[52] in her extensive study of newly promoted business leaders, reported that the new leaders found these multiple, sometimes contradictory, and often conflicting expectations the most perplexing part of their entry into leadership roles. Even those leaders who rose from the ranks within an organisation, such as Janice Burnley, often found that the expectations and demands of former colleagues and superiors in the system conflicted with personal expectations of how to do the job of principal.

'Outbound' trajectories

Janice's principal, Ken Sutton, actively attended to his 'outbound' trajectory by preparing Janice, his department heads, teaching staff, and his superiors in the district, for his eventual retirement from Lord Byron. His planning and intercession with system officials enabled Janice to succeed him with a minimum of disruption to the school. His foresight in planning for his own departure is quite different from the outbound trajectories of most of the school leaders we studied. Either as a result of poor planning by the school district, such as in the departures of Charmaine Watson from Talisman Park or Bill Andrews from Stewart Heights, or personal ambition, such as Bruce Grey's departure form Lord Byron, few leaders had the time, or took the time, to consolidate their legacy before they moved on.

The key to sustaining a leader's legacy appears to be the quality of the leadership left behind. At Lord Byron Wayne had often said he would know it was time to leave when he had "worked himself out of a job." To this end he encouraged and distributed leadership widely and as mentioned previously spawned an entire generation of leaders that greatly influenced the entire school district.

This was yet another lesson I had learned from Wayne. As principal at Watson, I worked very hard to make sure I had quality people in leadership roles. I lobbied the district to get the best assistant principal possible, and when opportunities to replace department heads came up, I ensured that these new leaders' commitment and values were consistent with the school's directions. Perhaps the most challenging part of leaders' 'outbound' trajectories is how to replace themselves. While such decisions are not fully in the hands of leaders, they can lobby the decision makers and usually have an influence. When I knew that I was to receive a promotion and leave Watson, I felt that someone with a very strong curriculum and teaching background should follow me. The assistant principal had already provided exemplary management and people skills, but the school needed to persist in developing and teaching a challenging program to all the students. I succeeded in convincing the district officials to assign my former colleague, Wally, to Watson High School. He was a masterful teacher and a powerful 'leader of learning' and turned out to be the perfect person for the job at that point in the school's evolution. He not only preserved the best aspects of what I had been able to do, but he pushed the school much further in terms of challenging students and teachers to excel.

This is an example of successful leadership succession that occurred many years ago and was more the product of good fortune than good management. Unfortunately, this pattern of serendipitous leadership succession persists today in education in most western educational authorities, especially in those schools in which local councils or governors chose new leaders. Educational jurisdictions continue to view investment in succession management as a cost and continue to 'hire and hope' that somehow new leaders will work out. Considering the importance of leadership to schools and districts and student learning, it seems ludicrous to perpetuate dated practices and attitudes and continue to just 'muddle' through. There are promising 'stirrings' of activity such as the National College for School

Leadership that seems intent on connecting the identification, recruitment, development, selection and on-going support of leaders into a coherent approach to succession management, but such efforts and investments are 'beacons' in a vast ocean of inaction.

Notes

1 This chapter looks at succession from an individual's perspective. See Hargreaves and Fink (2005) op.cit. for a comprehensive discussion of the topic from a school and system perspective.

2 Fulmer, R. and Conger, J. (2004). *Growing Your Companies' Leaders: How great organizations use succession management to sustain competitive advantage*. New York: Amacom, p. 2.

3 Rothwell, W.J. (2001). *Effective Succession Planning: Ensuring leadership continuity and building talent from within* (2nd edition). New York: Amacom, p. 5.

4 Eastman, L.J. (1995). *Succession Planning: An annotated bibliography and summary of commonly reported organizational practices*. Greensboro, NC: Center for Creative Leadership. p. 54.

5 Government of Western Australia (2001). 'Managing succession in the Western Australia public sector', at www.mpc.wa.gov.au

6 National Academy of Public Administration (1997). *Managing Succession and Developing Leadership: Growing the next generation of public service leaders*. Washington, DC: NAPA, p. 7.

7 Rothwell (2001) op. cit., p. 7.

8 Ibid, p. 7.

9 Wahl, A. (2004). 'Leaders wanted', *Canadian Business, 77* (5): pp. 31–5.

10 Byham, W.C. (2001). 'Grooming next-millennium leaders', *Society for Human Resources*, at www.shrm.org/articles.

11 Schall, E. (1997). 'Public sector succession: A strategic approach to sustaining innovation', *Public Administration Review, 57* (1): pp. 4–10; Liebman, M. and Bruer, R.A. (1994) 'Where there's a will there is a way', *Journal of Business Strategy,* 15 (2): pp. 26–34; National Academy of Public Administration, op. cit., 1997.

12 Eastman (1995) op. cit.; Souque, J.P. (1998) *Succession Planning and Leadership Development*. Ottawa, ON: Conference Board of Canada; Rothwell (2001) op. cit.

13 Institute for Educational Leadership (IEL) Task Force on the Principalship (2001). *Leadership for Student Learning: Redefining the teacher as leader*. Washington, DC: Institute for Educational Leadership, p. 1.

14 NAPA (1997) op. cit.; Langford, J., Vakii, T. and Lindquist, E.A. (2000). 'Tough challenges and practical solutions', *A Report on Con-*

ference Proceedings. Victoria: School of Public Administration, University of Victoria (www.futurework.telus.com/proceedings.pdf); Jackson, K. (2000) 'Building new teams: The next generation', a presentation at *The Future of Work in the Public Sector Conference*, organised by the School of Public Administration, University of Victoria, Victoria, BC, at www.futurework.telus.com/proceedings.pdf; Government of Western Australia (2001) op. cit.

15 Financial Executive International (FEI) (2001). *Building Human Capital: The public sector's 21st century challenge*, at www.fei.org

16 Langford et al. (2000) op. cit.

17 Government of Western Australia (2001) op. cit.

18 FEI (2001) op. cit.

19 Schall (1997) op. cit.

20 Jackson (2000) op. cit.

21 A. Levy, quoted in Jackson, I. and Nelson, J. (2004). *Profits with Principles: Seven strategies for delivering value with values*. New York: Doubleday, p. 109.

22 Pounder, D.G. and Young, P. (1996). 'Recruitment and Selection of Educational Administrators: Priorities for today's schools', in K. Leithwood, J. Chapman, D. Corson, P. Hallinger and A.W. Hart (eds), *International Handbook of Educational Leadership and Administration*. Netherlands: Kluwer Academic Publishers, pp. 279–308; Normore, A.H. (2001) *Recruitment, Socialization, and Accountability of School Administrators in Two School Districts*. An unpublished doctoral dissertation at the Ontario Institute for Studies in Education, University of Toronto.

23 Whatley, W. (1994). 'The extent to which teachers' impressions of new principals are influenced by experiences with and reactions to previous principals', Doctoral dissertation, University of South Carolina, 1994. Dissertation Abstracts International, 9508178. Hart, A.W. (1993) *Principal Succession: Establishing leadership in schools*. Albany, NY: SUNY Press. Warren, P. (1989) 'The First Year of Four Elementary Principals'. Unpublished M. Ed.

24 Wanous, J.P. (1980). *Organizational Entry: Recruitment, selection and socialization of school administration*. Reading, MA: Addison-Wesley Publishing Company; Pounder et al., op. cit.

25 Boesse, B. (1991). 'Planning how to transfer principals: A Manitoba experience', *Education Canada*, 31 (1): pp. 16–21; Aquila, F.D. (1989) 'Routine Principal Transfers Invigorate School Management', *Executive Educator*; 11 (2): pp. 24–5; Stine, D.E. (1998) 'A Change of Administration: A significant organizational life event'. Paper presented at the annual meeting of the American Educational Research Association, San Diego, CA, April; Hart, A.W. (1993) *Principal Succession: Establishing leadership in schools*. Albany, NY: SUNY Press.

26 Stoll, Fink, and Earl (2002) op. cit.

27 Schall (1997) op. cit., p. 4.

28 Wenger, op. cit.

29 Moss Kanter, R. (2004). *Confidence: How winning and losing streaks begin and end.* New York: Crown Business, pp. 3–25.

30 Hill, L.A. (2003). *Becoming a Manager: How new managers master the challenges of leadership.* Boston, MA: Harvard Business Press.

31 Smith, S. and Piele, P. (1989). *School Leadership: Handbook for excellence*, (2nd edition). Denver, CO: ERIC Clearing House on Educational Management, College of Education.

32 Baltzell, D.C. and Dentler, R.A. (1992). 'Five paths to principalship', in C. Marshall (ed.), *Women as School Administrators.* Indianapolis, IN: *Phi Delta Kappa*, (p. 5–9).

33 The first Director of the Halton Board of Education. See the Introduction.

34 Mintzberg, op. cit.

35 See Chapter 6.

36 McCall, M. (1988). 'Developing executive through work experience', *Human Resources Planning*, 11 (1): pp. 1–11.

37 McCall, ibid, p. 9.

38 Aquila, op. cit.; Boesse, op. cit.

39 Macmillan, R. (2000). 'Leadership succession, cultures of teaching and educational change', in A. Hargreaves and N. Bascia (eds), *The Sharp Edge of Educational Change.* London: Falmer, p. 68.

40 Raelin, J. (2000). *Work-Based Learning: The new frontier of management development.* Upper Saddle River, NJ: Prentice-Hall, p. 204.

41 McCall, op. cit., p. 4.

42 Mintzberg, op. cit, p. 211.

43 Ibid, p. 215.

44 Mintzberg, op. cit., p. 228.

45 See Mintzberg, ibid. He argues passionately that an MBA degree is much more meaningful to an experienced business leader.

46 Stoll and Fink (1996) op. cit., p. 85.

47 See Fink (2000) op. cit.

48 For an extended discussion of the 'loser' mentality, see Moss Kanter's study of winning and losing teams and organisations in Moss Kanter (2004) op. cit.

49 Ibid, p. 94.

50 Wenger, E., McDermott, R. and Snyder, W.M. (2002). 'Seven principles for cultivating communities of practice', in *Harvard Business School Working Knowledge.* e-mail newsletter (25 March), at http://hbsworkingknowledge.hbs.edu/item.jhtml?id=2855&t=organizations

51 The mere mention of Lord Byron was another mistake.

52 Hill, L.A. (2003). *Becoming a Manager: How new managers master the challenges of leadership.* Boston, MA: Harvard Business School Press.

Conclusion

Many years ago, one of my former teachers' college instructors, a rather cryptic and sardonic Scot named Jock Carlisle, used to tell us "You need some conclusion to your lesson other than the bell", and suggested that we leave the students with two or three thought-provoking ideas that would link into the next day's lesson. In memory of Jock, I leave you with these summarising principles of *Leadership for Mortals*.

Leaders of learning are ordinary people who through extraordinary commitment, effort, and determination have become extraordinary, and have made the people around them exceptional.

Educational leadership is more art than science; it is more about character than technique; it is more about inspiration than charisma; it is more about leading student and teacher learning than the management of things.

Leaders must be passionately, creatively, obsessively and steadfastly committed to enhancing 'deep' learning for students – learning for understanding, learning for life, learning for a knowledge society.

Leadership is about communicating invitational messages to individuals and groups with whom the leader interacts in order to build and act on a shared and evolving vision of a *learning-centred* school.

We all have the ability to shape events in our lives as opposed to being shaped by circumstances. To embrace this ability, leaders must enhance and employ all of their qualities – reason, ethics, imagination, intuition, memory and common sense – in equilibrium.

The capacity of a leader or someone else to identify with an organisation and for these leaders to negotiate a shared sense of direction for the school or district with their staff(s) will depend in large measure on the trajectory that determines the leader's form of participation or non-participation in an organisation's various 'communities of practice'.

School systems need to define leadership roles flexibly in terms of what will be required in the future rather than limiting role descriptions to existing competencies.

I saw my first major league baseball game in Cleveland with my Dad and my Uncle Dean. The pitcher was a 46 year old rookie named Satchel Paige. Although acknowledged as one of the greatest baseball pitchers in America, he never had a chance to play in the 'Big Leagues' because, as a black man, he was excluded. Long past his prime he still led the Cleveland team to victory in the World Series.[1] A sharecropper's son he was not well educated but wise in his own way. He used to say

> Work like you don't need the money.
> Love like you've never been hurt.
> Dance like nobody's watching.[2]

I would amend this slightly to suggest that

> Teach and lead like ours is the most important profession in
> the world.

> Because it is.

We touch the face of the future. Ours is a hope profession. We don't depend on society's failures for business. Every little child that walks through our school-house door is a hope for the future. The late Neil Postman captured this very well when he said

> Children are the living messages that we send to a time we will
> not see.[3]

Notes

[1] A pitcher is like a bowler in cricket, and the World Series is the ultimate contest in baseball.

[2] 'Wise and Wiser', *Sports Illustrated*, July, 16, 2000, p. 34.

[3] Postman, N. (1984). *The Disappearance of Childhood*. New York: Vintage Books, p.xi.

Author index

Subject index